North Weald was home to these 111 Squadron Hunter F.4s at the time of this photo, in 1956. (Key)

Neville Duke at the controls of the Hunter prototype WB188, during an early test flight. (Key)

FOREWORD

I was delighted on being asked to compile this history of the Hawker Hunter for Key Publishing's now firmly established Combat Machines series. It is timed to coincide with the release of Airfix's new-tool 1/48 Hunter kit, but it will also appeal to the pure aviation enthusiast. Delight, because the Hunter has long been one of my favourites, but it is also considered one of the most successful and popular British fighters of all time. If that is not enough, it was and still is one of the world's best-looking military aeroplanes.

This work presents a general history of the type and covers its design and development, test flying, different production versions and a review of an extensive and successful service and combat career, both with home and overseas air arms (the latter providing large-scale exports fo industry). Further spe explore trials and research airframes, and display teams, and there are memories of a former pilot who flew the aircraft with 20 Squadron RAF.

The Hunter was unable to go supersonic in level flight, but in a dive it could pass through the mythical 'sound barrier' with ease. It was a manoeuvrable aeroplane, could absorb rough handling and in general was revered by the many pilots who flew it. The type has been well served by books and magazine articles over the years, but these pages include new information and a large selection of previously unpublished and rare photographs, many of which are in colour and all of great value to modellers. I hope readers will like the result.

Tony Buttler AMRAeS
Author

A fine Air Ministry study of Armstrong Siddeley Sapphire-powered Hunter F.5 WP183, built by Armstrong Whitworth and wearing 56 Squadron RAF markings. (Crown Copyright)

Hunter FGA.9s of 208 Squadron, from Eastleigh, Kenya, formate near Mt Kilimanjaro. The right-hand aircraft, XE607, crashed during an open day at Khormaksar, Aden, on March 29, 1962. The subsequent report blamed a runaway tailplane trim fault for the accident. (Key)

Author: Tony Buttler AMRAeS
Series Editor: Chris Clifford
Acknowledgements: The primary references used for this work included Avia and Air files in the National Archives at Kew, and flight test reports and documents at the Brooklands Museum. For serial data the author referred mostly to Hawker Hunter 1951 to 2008 In UK and Foreign Service by David J Griffin, while unit information was accessed mainly from Air-Britain's The Squadrons of the Royal Air Force & Commonwealth 1918-1988, by James Halley. Further information on the Hunter's design and development programme can be found in the author's own book The Design and Development of the Hawker Hunter (History Press 2014)
Colour artwork: Andy Hay – Flying Art
Designer: Tom Bagley
Group Designer: Steve Donovan
Group Editor: Stuart Qualtrough
Production Manager: Janet Watkins
Commercial Director: Ann Saundry
Group CEO and Publisher: Adrian Cox

Key Publishing Ltd: PO Box 100, Stamford, Lincolnshire, PE9 1XQ, United Kingdom.
Distributed by: Seymour Distribution Ltd, 2 Poultry Avenue, London, EC1A 9PP.
Tel: 020 7429 4000. Fax: 020 7429 4001.
Printed by: Warners (Midland) plc, Bourne.
Printed in England
ISBN: 978-1-912205-752

COLD WAR NECESSITY

A beautiful Ministry of Supply study of a highly attractive aircraft…the first Hawker Hunter prototype, WB188. (Phil Butler)

Development of the Hawker Hunter began in 1946, when the Air Staff raised a Specification and Operational Requirement, F.43/46 and OR.228, for a new day interceptor fighter designed to destroy high-speed, high-flying enemy bombers.

This new type would replace the wartime Gloster Meteor, but such was the speed of advance in aerodynamics, technology and weaponry during the late 1940s that by February 1948, the Specification had to be updated and was renumbered F.3/48.

In the meantime, Hawker Aircraft's designers at Kingston, under Sydney Camm, had looked closely at what was needed to make an ideal interceptor. The team concentrated particularly in achieving the smallest possible frontal area with a single engine (some F.43/46 design proposals had two engines). This effort culminated in a design called the P.1067, and in fact, F.3/48 was essentially written around this Hawker project. Issued in October 1948, it called for a maximum speed of 547kts (630mph/1,014km/h) at 45,000ft (13,716m). The powerplant was to be a single Rolls-Royce Avon or Armstrong Siddeley Sapphire turbojet, while armament was to comprise two or four 30mm Aden cannon.

Refinement

In August 1948 the P.1067 design had a tubular fuselage with a circular nose intake and a T-tail, the latter being considered the best from an aerodynamic perspective. In January 1949 it was agreed that the first two P.1067s should have an Avon engine with a Sapphire going in the third. Two months later, an ever-increasing equipment load meant that a nose air intake was no longer possible. This serious hurdle was solved by the introduction of a solid nose and a bifurcated wing root intake, an alteration cleared officially in January 1949. Apart from its T-tail, the P.1067 looked like a Hunter and as such, a part-complete full-size mock-up of this form was inspected officially in August. Finally, in October 1949, the tailplane was moved to the lower position on the fin, thus completing the Hunter's

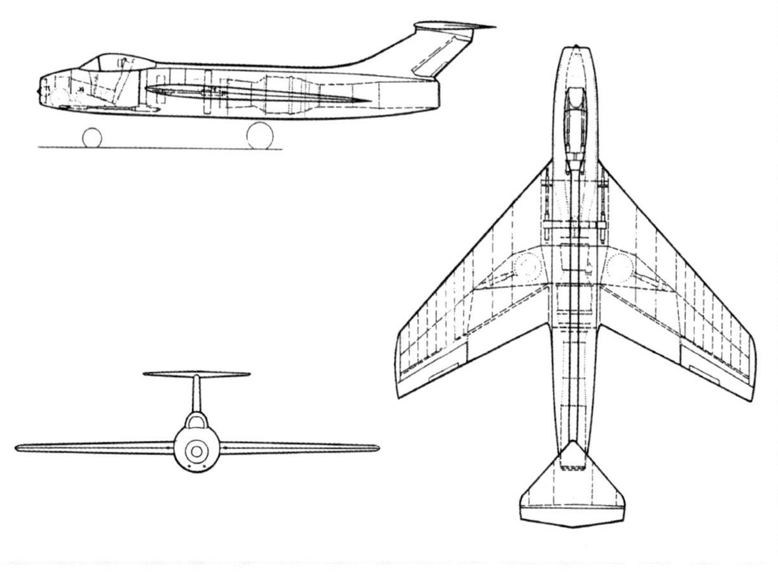

The Hawker P.1067 as it appeared in August 1948, when still sporting a nose intake. (Phil Butler)

configuration as one of the most graceful aeroplanes ever built.

In addition to its wind tunnel research, Hawker had been accumulating valuable flight test data. The firm's first jet fighter was the straight wing and very successful naval Sea Hawk, first flown as the P.1040 in September 1947. Subsequently, two modified Sea Hawk airframes, serials VX272 and VX279, were completed with swept wings as P.1052s, so the manufacturer could garner first-hand experience of swept flying surfaces. VX272 first flew on November 19, 1948, but this pair retained the Sea Hawk's straight tailplane.

During May and June 1950, VX279 was rebuilt as the P.1081 with a new swept tail and all-through jet pipe, which gave a handsome layout of similar configuration to the Hunter but keeping the Sea Hawk's more rounded body. Hawker Chief Test Pilot Sqn Ldr Trevor 'Wimpy' Wade took VX279 on its maiden flight in this new layout on June 19, 1950, and the aircraft was painted in a pale duck egg green scheme characteristic of several Hawker prototypes of this period. Hawker's own P.1081 flight trials ended in February 1951 and the pilots reported how delighted they were with the aircraft. At its full fighter weight, VX279 had displayed exceptional performance, virtually viceless handling characteristics, good manoeuvrability and a controllable Mach number up to at least 0.94.

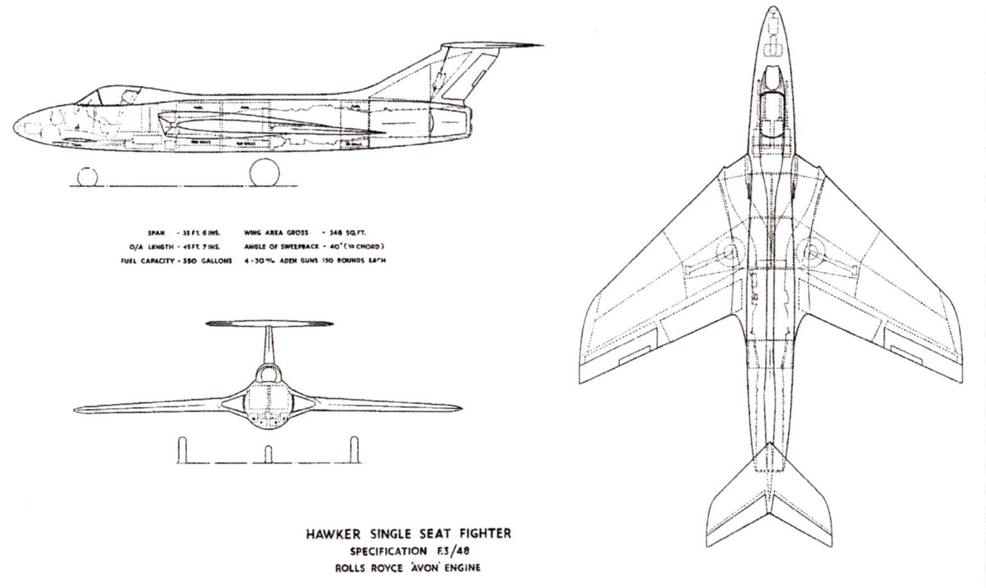

How the Hawker P.1067 looked in May 1949. A solid nose and root intakes were introduced but a T-tail was still present. This design was part-built as a full-size mock-up. Its span was 33ft 6in (10.2m), length 45ft 7in (13.9m) and wing area 348 sq ft (32.36m²). (All Tony Buttler unless stated)

In fact, it was considered superior to any other British aircraft then flying but tragically, before official trials could begin, Wade lost his life and VX279 was destroyed in a flying accident on April 3, 1951. Wade and the P.1081 had, however, done much to confirm that the final layout chosen for the Hunter was good.

At this stage the P.1067 had no name. A British national newspaper contest had selected 'Demon', but the American Navy's new McDonnell F3H interceptor, flown in August 1951, had already taken this moniker and so 'Hunter' was picked instead, and announced officially to the public in March 1952. In October 1950, well before the first P.1067 had flown, a production order for 200 airframes was placed as part of an expansion programme for the RAF…brought about by the outbreak of war in Korea. The first versions were to be the F.1 powered by a Rolls-Royce Avon RA.7 and the F.2 with an Armstrong Siddeley Sapphire Sa.6.

Early flying

The two Avon-powered prototypes carried the serials WB188 and WB195, while the Sapphire-powered machine was serialled WB202. Hunter WB188, unarmed and again in duck-egg green, began taxi trials at the Aircraft and Armament Experimental Establishment (A&AEE) at Boscombe Down, on July 8, 1951. It made

Hunter WB188 without guns fitted, before the aircraft's maiden flight.

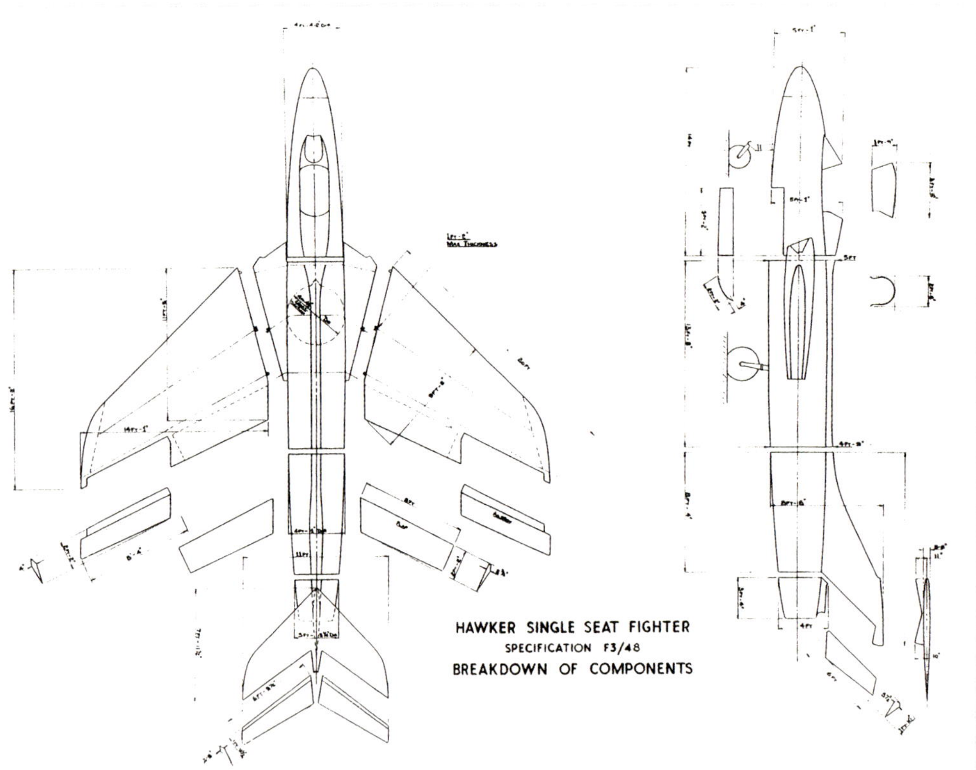

A drawing dated July 1949, showing the component breakdown for the T-tail version. For the Hunter as built this would have been quite similar. (National Archives)

its debut flight from Boscombe on July 20 with Sqn Ldr Neville Duke in the cockpit, Duke having succeeded Wade as chief test pilot. In September he took WB188 to the Society of British Aircraft Constructors' show at Farnborough for its first public demonstration, where he recorded the highest speeds achieved thus far by any aircraft displayed at any Farnborough, and often just tens of feet above the runway. WB188 was then grounded between October and January 1952 for modifications to the fin and rudder, to try and stop vibration that had appeared as the flight speeds increased. Duke took the P.1067 through the 'sound barrier' for the first time in April 1952.

WB195 was the first prototype to have the four 30mm Aden gun pack and had its maiden flight on May 5, 1952. It was demonstrated at the September 1952 Farnborough and in December went to Boscombe Down for appraisal. However, heavy vibration caused by elevator flutter was experienced when pulling out from a dive at low altitude and high speed, and WB195 then became involved in extended flutter trials to solve this problem; these lasted until December 1953.

In December 1952 work began on fitting WB188 with wing fuel tanks and a 9,500lb (42.2kN) thrust Avon RA.7R with reheat, as the sole Hunter Mk.3 (or sometimes F.3). It was repainted in a bright scarlet scheme and produced as a one-off for reheat development trials (to improve the rate of climb and acceleration) and as a test aircraft for the P.1083 supersonic Hunter described later. WB188's maiden flight in this form was made on July 7, 1953, but the powerplant provided insufficient improvement in level flight speed and Camm decided that reheat's extra weight, complexity and cost was

This photo of the Hawker P.1081 prototype shows its swept wing and tail and all-through jet pipe… features all employed on the Hunter. (Jo Ware)

not worthwhile. A higher thrust 'dry' engine would be better suited for the Hunter, which in due course appeared as the Series 200 Avon.

That said, on September 7, 1953, Duke used WB188 to set a new level flight world speed record of 727.6mph (1,170.7km/h). Although in almost all respects a standard airframe, WB188 then had a curved, highly raked fairing over the existing windscreen, and a pointed nose. The aircraft was based at Tangmere for the record attempt and the new figure was calculated as a mean of four separate speed runs, two in each direction, over a 3km course near Littlehampton in Sussex. A second speed record fell to Duke and WB188 on September 19, the 100km closed circuit, which at the time did not necessarily capture the popular imagination as did the air speed record, but for a fighter type for the RAF it was more significant. The recorded speed of 709.2mph (1,141.1km/h) was made in relatively poor weather conditions, around a course that started and ended at Hawker's Dunsfold airfield. It embraced a 25-mile (40.2km) straight outward leg, a 12-mile (19.3km) turn and then another 25-mile (40.2km) straight run home.

On retirement WB188 was used for ground instruction with serial 7154M and the prototype is now preserved, still in red, at the Tangmere Military Aviation Museum. Later in its career, WB195 was used for barrier trials and ground instruction with the serial 7284M and was not sold for scrap until 1967. The Sapphire-powered and silver-painted WB202 began its flying programme on November 30, 1952, and from mid-February 1953 was used for gun-firing trials. In March 1953, WB202 was fitted with an extended fin to provide improved stability, a successful modification applied to all subsequent Hunters. The aircraft was displayed at the 1954 SBAC Show, and in 1956 it took part in crash barrier trials, but was then used for fire-fighting practice and scrapped in 1960.

Development problems

Difficulties with firing the guns was one of the issues experienced during the programmes to clear the Hunter for service use. These were caused by surging in the Avon engine and came to light in late 1954. The powerplant would stall when the guns were fired at high altitude, though not every time. Early 100-series Avons had proved touchy when it came to surge because there was very little margin, and solving this critical problem took considerable time. However, a short-term solution was to 'dip' (reduce) the fuel supply just milliseconds before firing, which made a two second burst at five-second intervals possible without surge.

However, the operational effectiveness of the Avon marks was not good enough; the Ministry of

▲ For its early flights the first Hunter prototype had a spin recovery parachute housing positioned above the jet orifice, as visible here. (Phil Butler)

▼ Neville Duke sits inside his bright red-painted record-breaking Hunter Mk.3.

WB202 comes into land, probably at Farnborough. Note the deployed flaps and undercarriage doors.

Supply (MoS) was not happy and Rolls-Royce designer Adrian Lombard met ministry chief Reginald Maudling to find something better. A further round of engine development followed, which lasted until the summer of 1956 and involved modifications to the Avon compressor. In addition, the Royal Aircraft Establishment (RAE) at Farnborough produced a modification that enabled the four guns to be fired slightly out of synchronization, thereby reducing the effects of their blast (the blast of the four Aden cannon was so powerful it had damaged several nose components, such as the nosewheel rod, while another effect had been a nose-down pitch when the guns were fired at high altitude). These changes essentially cured the gun firing problem and modified engines were tested in Hunters WT573, WT574, WT612, WT736 and WV276. The later Hunter F.6 with 200-series Avon had a much-improved surge margin and never experienced any worries with gun operation.

Well before first flight, the MoS had warned Hawker of the need to ensure spent gun cartridges and links would have to be ejected clear of the aircraft. However, by July 1954 spent shell cases from firing trails were damaging the air brake because the deflector plates used thus far were just not effective enough. Hawker subsequently devised a scheme that employed two streamlined fairings fixed to the underside, beneath the cockpit, to collect the links and expended shells and these became a feature of production Hunters. The fairings were nicknamed 'Sabrinas', echoing the alias of a popular British glamour model of the period, Norma Ann Sykes.

The first two Hunter marks also suffered from a lack of fuel and endurance. This was addressed by two new Hunter versions, the Avon-powered F.4 and the Sapphire-equipped F.5, both of which carried more internal fuel and a drop tank beneath each wing. The fuel worry came into stark focus on February 8, 1956, when eight F.1s from the Day Fighter Leader School, at Norfolk's RAF West Raynham, took off for a combat exercise. The weather then closed in at their home base and the group had to recover to RAF Marham (in the same county) under ground radar control, but confusion ensued, the Hunter's landing approaches became stretched and just two of the fighters were able to land safely. The other six all crashed and tragically one of the pilots was killed. These early

Views showing the different jetpipes of WB188 and WB202, and an early airbrake arrangement on the former aircraft. (Chris Goss/Key)

Hunters had run out of fuel after just 40-45mins.

The P.1067/Hunter was originally designed to also use its wing landing flaps for air or dive brakes. In November 1952, however, Sydney Camm reported that these airbrakes were proving ineffective at high speeds, while in the landing configuration they had caused large and possibly unacceptable changes of trim. Then in December the Hunter went to Boscombe Down for handling trials and the establishment's pilots found they did not like the airbrakes at all, declaring they were unacceptable. Throughout 1953 and into 1954 the inadequacy of the Hunter airbrakes was another major problem, and in November 1953 the Air Staff stated that it would not accept the Hunter unless it was provided with effective airbrakes, which could be used safely throughout the aircraft's speed and Mach number range.

But it was not until February 1954 that the flap dive brake format was finally abandoned by Hawker, when at about the same time a new under-fuselage airbrake was produced. The airbrake trials, employing many available production aircraft, included the following two arrangements:

a) Fuselage brakes with the holes in the fuselage behind the brakes filled in, and with horizontal fins fitted to the top and bottom of the brakes, and to the fuselage opposite the brakes. The object of this modification was to negate the turbulence due to the holes in the fuselage, and to prevent the air flow from the brakes interfering with the tailplane.

b) A new type of rear fuselage brake fitted to an aircraft with a production-type jet pipe. These brakes were fitted lower down the sides of the fuselage.

Originally the fuselage brakes were designed to be fitted at the extreme aft fuselage near the jet pipe, but they were in fact installed on one of the prototype Hunters that had a jet pipe some 18in (45cm) shorter than on production machines, ie. it was 18in nearer to the brakes. Flight trials in autumn 1953 revealed these brakes caused considerable buffet, and an unacceptable nose-down change of trim, and this was thought to be due to the proximity of the jet efflux; Hawker subsequently moved the brakes approximately 1ft (30cm) further forward.

Fortunately, the decision taken shortly after mid-summer 1953 not to fit reheat to the Hunter made the addition of fuselage air brakes easier. An under-fuselage airbrake, which was considered acceptable by service pilots, was tested in February-March 1954, though in its original form it did not produce adequate deceleration

Hunter F.1 WT631 displays the prominent underfuselage airbrake eventually fitted to all production Hunters.

At one stage WB202 carried dummy de Havilland Firestreak air-to-air missiles. (Phil Butler)

An official Ministry photo of the first production Hawker Hunter, serial WT555. (Phil Butler)

and further development work was still required. Finally, after lengthy experimentation, the external 'barn door' underneath the rear fuselage became standard.

Hawker built the Hunter F.1s and F.4s, while Coventry-based Armstrong Whitworth was awarded contracts to produce F.2s and F.5s. Hunter production also became a subject of the British Government's 'Superpriority' scheme, intended to improve the speed of production of several new fighters, bombers and other types. Following a rundown within the aircraft industry, with a loss of facilities and skilled labour, new types such as the Hunter and the V-Bombers, entering production at roughly the same time, had presented big problems with capacity and capability. Superpriority was intended to clear the bottlenecks, but in terms of a general acceleration of production it was only partially successful.

Intensive trials

Hawker test pilot Frank Murphy took WT555, the first production F.1, on its maiden flight on May 16, 1953, and the first 20 F.1s were all used in various trials programmes. Between May and September 1954, three more F.1s undertook the type's intensive flying trials, but the first production mark fell short of the performance figures outlined by F.3/48, being very poor on time-to-height and ceiling (worse in fact than the Soviet Mikoyan MiG-15) and short on endurance and maximum speed. The Hawker Hunter F.1 received its Controller (Aircraft) C(A) Release to Service in July 1954, but with several limitations, including restrictions to gun firing until the trials and modifications already described had been completed. Although falling short of F.3/48's requirements, because of its overall higher level of performance the Hunter had made a generally favourable impression and represented a considerable advance on previous British operational fighters.

A mid-1954 A&AEE review of the F.1 noted that for handling, the main attributes were generally docile transonic handling characteristics, excellent aileron control and a reasonably ergonomic cockpit layout. But at this stage these positive attributes were marred by the rapid pitch up in manoeuvres at high subsonic Mach numbers, and by the elevator becoming excessively heavy in that scenario. Trials with a fully powered elevator eventually brought considerable improvement in longitudinal control, and this was recommended as an interim solution.

WN888, the first production F.2 and the first Hunter from Armstrong Whitworth, initially flew from Baginton airfield near Coventry, on October 14, 1953. In the cockpit was Armstrong Whitworth chief test pilot Eric Franklin, and superficially the Mks.1 and 2 were near identical. However, there was a small but clear distinction. Both had a small flush intake above the port side of the engine bay, but on the F.2 an oil-vent outlet was visible just forward of and below this point. Early F.2s were again used for trials and the F.2 C(A) Service Release was awarded in August 1954, but with similar restrictions to the F.1, though in general the Sapphire-powered machines had experienced fewer teething troubles than the Avon Hunters.

▼ Hunter F.4, WV327/U, 222 Squadron RAF, Leuchars, Fife. Dark Green, Dark Sea Grey, High Speed Silver.

▼ Hunter FGA.9, XF445/R, 43 Squadron RAF. Established lists do not state this aircraft as being on strength with 43 Squadron, but the markings clearly show otherwise. Dark Green, Dark Sea Grey, and Light Aircraft Grey.

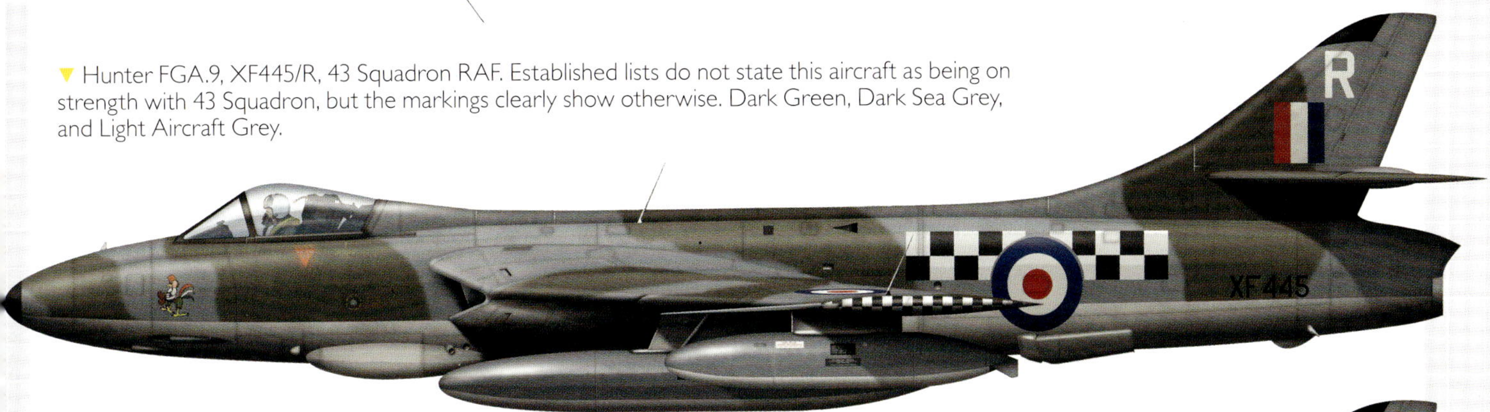

▼ Hunter F.6, XF462, CO of 66 Squadron RAF, Acklington. Dark Green, Dark Sea Grey and High Speed Silver.

▼ Hunter F.6, XF383/14, 229 OCU/145 'Shadow' Squadron RAF, Chivenor, June 1961. Dark Green, Dark Sea Grey, High Speed Silver.

▼ Hunter FGA.9, XE622/A, 28 Squadron RAF, Kai Tak, Hong Kong, 1966. Dark Green, Dark Sea Grey, Light Aircraft Grey.

(Andy Hay/www.flyingart.co.uk)

Three F.1s from 43 Squadron – WT594/U nearest, WT622/G (fitted with 'Sabrina' link collectors) and WT641/T. Note the unusual position of the rear fuselage code letters. (Crown Copyright)

VARIANTS IN SERVICE

The Hawker Hunter joined the RAF in 1954 and equipped many of the service's squadrons and a host of support units in the UK, in RAF Germany and in the Middle and Far East. Some Royal Navy squadrons also flew the aircraft and this section explores the Hunter's UK air arm service. Display flying, research activity and the Hunter's considerable involvement in various wars and conflicts overseas are described later.

A 263 Squadron F.2, serial WN946/N. (Brian Wallis via Roger Lindsay)

F.1 and F.2

Trials and evaluation work kept busy the first 20 production F.1s. The debut RAF unit to be equipped with the F.1 was 43 Squadron at Leuchars, Fife. Its very first Hunter, WW599, was delivered from 5 Maintenance Unit at Kemble, Gloucestershire, on July 29, 1954, though 43's operational flying with the Hunter did not commence until mid-September as it gradually replaced its Gloster Meteor F.8 fighters. To begin with, the squadron's primary role was to perform intensive trials with its new mount, under operational conditions. For example, in January 1956 it carried out firing trials with new high-velocity 30mm ammunition, and in doing so the unit uncovered and/or confirmed the F.1's various weaknesses.

This sub-type did, however, display many worthy features. One was its short turn-round time after a sortie. In February 1955 the aviation press watched groundcrews remove the gun panels from one machine, detach the barrels of the four Aden guns, lower the huge gun pack onto a trolley before replacing the barrels, winching up a new fully re-armed pack (weighing 1,900lb/862kg), recharging the oxygen bottles, replacing the gun's cine film, and finally completing the Hunter's refuelling in just 5 mins 42 secs.

In addition, the Hunter provided its pilots with substantially increased performance. Having struggled to intercept the Canberra bomber in

change from what had been possible with the Meteor.

After 43's debut, the F.1 joined 54, 222 and 247 Squadrons and these home-based units were the only frontline examples to fly this mark, although airframes also joined 229 and 233 OCUs (the Operational Conversion Units that trained new pilots for Hunter squadrons) and the Day Fighter Leaders' School (part of the Central Fighter Establishment/ CFE). The F.1's lack of range was ably demonstrated by CFE when, shortly after acquiring its Hunters, several took part in Exercise Dividend. Here the Hunter could for the first time fly simulated interceptions against fast jet bombers flying at high altitude (USAF B-47 Stratojets and B-45 Tornados, and RAF Canberras) and it proved successful in this role. Critically, however, no interceptions were possible at distances beyond 80 miles (129km) from base, a serious weakness in such an important task.

This Hunter F.4, WV269/H of 74 Squadron, lifts off from Horsham St Faith during 1957's Exercise Vigilant. Note the whitewash identity panel applied to the tail for these wargames. This aircraft was scrapped at 5 Maintenance Unit, RAF Kemble, in June 1961. (Key)

practice for so long, they knew that such targets could no longer evade an attack. On top of this, in a transonic dive the Hunter could pass through into supersonic flight with considerable ease. A typical dive might start at around 40,000ft (12,192m) and it was possible for the pilot to aim his supersonic 'bang' at a chosen spot on the ground. The Hunter gave its first public demonstration of supersonic diving during a NATO air display held in Brussels, in July 1952, while on November 30, 1954, a German Parliament delegation visiting RAF Marham was treated to a spectacular performance. Flight magazine reported how: "Two Hunter F.1s from CFE took off as a close pair and proceeded to give a most exhilarating performance. One of them started a battle climb to gain altitude for a sonic boom, while the other roared sharply skywards and disappeared from view. After a few minutes' pause, the commentator announced over the loudspeaker that the sonic boom was due, and that the aircraft might possibly appear before the sound was heard. This in fact happened. The Hunter raced silently across Marham at several thousand feet and had passed the aerodrome by the time a thunderous double-clap shook the tower, followed immediately by the howl of the aircraft's passing. A thick double vapour puff was visible at approximately 10,000ft (3,048m). The second Hunter passed by at 50ft (15m) at full power, only just preceded by its characteristic roar." This was a sea-

A vary rare view of F.5 WN891, at the Central Experimental and Proving Establishment (CEPE), Rockcliff near Ottawa, or the Winter Experimental Establishment at Namao near Edmonton, both in Canada, during the type's 1955 'winterisation' trials. While there, WN891 was also displayed at the Namao Airshow. This aircraft never joined a squadron and was on the fire dump at Farnborough by 1959. (Key)

Hunter F.5 WP147 of 41 Squadron, which was based at Biggin Hill from 1955-58. (Key)

Twin-seat Hunter T.7 XL609 was allocated to 56 Squadron and is pictured at Wethersfield in 1962. (Terry Panopalis collection)

Just two squadrons flew the F.2, those being 257 (from September 1954) and 263, both again former Meteor operators. Further F.2s joined the Air Fighting Development Squadron (another CFE unit) during 1955, another (WN891) went to the Central Experimental and Proving Establishment (CEPE) in Canada for Hunter 'winterisation' testing, and two more were acquired temporarily by 1 Squadron. During their brief careers with the first two marks of Hunter, these squadrons also undertook a considerable amount of display and publicity flying, but by the close of 1956 the F.1 was no longer in the hands of any frontline unit, although some F.2s remained on strength until March 1957. Other examples of both marks were passed to training units or for ground instruction, but many went for scrap after very short lives.

F.4 and F.5

The first UK Fighter Command Squadron to re-equip with the longer-range F.4, from June 1955, was 111, which had been flying Meteor F.8s. It was quickly followed by 54 and 247 Squadrons, while the original Hunter unit, 43, and 222 Squadron, had completed their conversion to F.4 fighters by March 1956. Finally, by April the Canadair CL.13 Sabres serving with 66 and 92 Squadrons were replaced by the Hunter .4.

April 1955 also brought the arrival of the first Hunter F.5s, beginning with 263 Squadron. That May, 56 Squadron, which had previously been the only frontline unit to operate the early marks of the Hunter's direct rival, the Supermarine Swift, received its first F.5s. Other UK squadrons to covert to F.5s during 1955-56 were 1, 34, 41, 257 and 263, mostly as replacements for Meteors.

The extended endurance of the Hunter F.4 and 5 was shown to good effect very quickly during Fighter Command's annual Exercise Beware, held in late September 1955. This was an air defence exercise in which the participants would experience a simulated war situation. The Meteor F.8 had regularly been out-turned at height by the opposing Canberras, which could not only perform these evasion tactics but also follow up with quarter attacks on the Meteors themselves. The Hunters could now attack the Canberras from above, much to the delight and relief of their pilots! The aviation press reporting on Beware stressed: "that the new radar techniques and equipment, coupled with the indisputable success of the Hunter as an interceptor, have given Britain a vastly improved air defence".

This straight-winged F.6, XF449/S served with 19 and 92 Squadrons from 1957, and it received leading-edge extensions and gun blast deflectors retrospectively. (Crown Copyright)

Hunter F.6 XG164/H of 74 Squadron. Note the gun blast deflectors and 'H' on the forward nosewheel door. (Crown Copyright)

On August 5, 1955, Sqn Ldr Roger Topp, CO of 111 Squadron and who (as described later) would make his unit and its pilots famous for their display flying, flew a Hunter F.4 from Turnhouse, near Edinburgh, to Farnborough in Hampshire in just 29 mins 33.4 secs. This established a new (but unofficial) record and the average speed for the fight was around 680mph (1,094km/h). His achievement recalled, and was compared to, an effort made by an earlier Hawker product, a Hurricane, flying from Turnhouse to Northolt in 1938 (which took 48 mins at an average of 409mph/658km/h); here was a graphic illustration of the advances made possible by jet power. Topp followed the feat a few days later with a second Turnhouse-to-Farnborough run, this time in just 27 mins 46 secs for an average of 717mph (1,154km/h).

September 1956 brought the next annual Fighter Command exercise, Stronghold, in which 41 (F.5) and 247 (F.4) Squadrons took part. The competition between the two versions revealed the Sapphire engine used by the F.5 gave that variant a distinct edge when it came to scramble times. During Stronghold the Hunters also tangled with Dutch F-100 Super Sabres, against which they performed reasonably well, while the main targets were RAF Canberra and Valiant bombers and American B-47s. By autumn 1956 the Hunter had become fully established in RAF squadron service.

Although based in the UK, in 1956, 1 and 34 Squadrons were detached to Nicosia, Cyprus, to permit their aircraft to take part in the Suez Campaign, and which for recognition purposes the Hunters had prominent black and yellow stripes painted around their wings and rear fuselages. Later, Hunter F.6s and FGA.9s would also visit the Middle East and this early detachment provided useful experience when preparing for later excursions.

One more squadron, 74, converted to the F.4 in March 1957, but from January 1958 this unit began to switch to the F.6. Again, both F.4 and F.5 were to spend a relatively short time in the UK's front line as the F.6 came on stream. The year 1957 brought 257 Squadron's disbandment in March, and the same fate befell 222 in October and 247 in December, while 34 and 41 Squadrons were disbanded in January 1958. No F.4s remained in Fighter Command's front line by February 1958, while the last F.5 unit, 1 Squadron, disbanded

One of the few occasions, indeed possibly the only time, when UK-based Hunters had to use weapons in anger. On March 18, 1967, the British Petroleum-operated tanker SS *Torrey Canyon* ran aground and broke up on Seven Stones Reef, between Cornwall and the Isles of Scilly. Fleet Air Arm and RAF aircraft employed bombs, rockets, napalm and kerosene to burn off the crude oil. Here, diving from top-left, a 1 Squadron Hunter drops napalm on the slick. (Key)

F.6A XG225/27 of 1 TWU, based at Brawdy in 1979 and painted in an experimental high-visibility paint scheme. (Chris Goss)

in June that year. No 56 Squadron continued to use a mix of F.5s and F.6s until November 1958, after which it became an all-F.6 outfit. No F.5s were ever based permanently outside the UK.

F.6

The F.6 with its later Avon 203 engine was clearly superior to the F.1-5 and became very popular with its pilots. The Hunter's airframe design meant the new engine could not provide the F.6 with a definite increase in maximum speed at all altitudes over what had been achieved in the F.4, but elements such as its rate of climb at height were vastly improved (at 45,000ft [13,716m] for example the F.4 figure was 1,000ft/min [305m/min] when the F.6 recorded 1,700ft/min [518m/min]). The Avon 203's freedom from surging also eliminated the problems with gun firing at altitude; in June 1958 four 43 Squadron Hunters conducted an exercise where each F.6 fired all four guns twice at a height of 51,000ft (15,545m).

Unlike the English Electric Lightning's introduction in the early 1960s, when it would operate as an integrated all-weather weapons system, during the 1950s it was general Fighter Command policy to have two day fighter and one night fighter squadron forming a single wing at each operational airfield. The ascendance of Hunter F.6 squadrons was rapid, the first to acquire examples being 74 and, with a planned conversion rate of two squadrons per month, this unit was quickly followed by 19, 43, 54, 63, 65, 66, 74, 92, 111, 247 and 263 Squadrons; three of these, 19, 63 and 65, were still flying the Meteor F.8 rather than earlier Hunters. Non-operational RAF Hunter F.6 units included the Operational Conversion Units (229 and 233), CFE, the Fighter Weapons School, Central Flying School and Empire Test Pilots' School.

Although it was only capable of subsonic speed horizontally, the Hunter's rate of climb, agility and dive speed had enabled the fighter to intercept the British Canberra, and the American B-45 and B-47 bombers, with little trouble…all of which flew at heights between 35,000ft and 43,000ft (10,668m and 13,106m). This was important because similar frontline bomber types were currently in service with the Soviet Air Force, but the forthcoming RAF V-Bombers (Vulcan, Victor and Valiant) would be another matter altogether.

This first became evident during a major NATO operation called Exercise Strikeback, a multi-national and multi-air arm affair held in the north and mid-Atlantic over ten

In the late 1950s, T.7 trainer XL586 flew with 226 Operational Conversion Unit as 'RS/90'. (Crown Copyright)

Hunter F.6A XF418/16, also with 1 TWU at Brawdy in 1979, displaying an alternative red high-vis paint scheme, which also formed part of the trial. This aircraft has also been photographed with a replacement camouflaged tail cone. (Chris Goss)

days in September 1957. For the Hunters involved, again the principal targets were Canberras and B-47s, against which they coped well, but the first of the V-Bombers, the Vickers Valiant, also took part and this aircraft's operational ceiling of 49,000ft (14,935m) gave it a valuable extra margin in which to evade the attacking fighters. Both Vulcan and Victor were expected to fly even higher and with even more performance, and the Avro bomber began to play its part in exercises towards the end of 1957. Because their mounts were only marginally faster at height than either Vulcan or Victor, Hunter pilots discovered that making a successful interception was especially difficult unless they could establish an advantage in both speed and height. This was a near-impossible situation because the first marks of both of these V-types had operational ceilings in the region of 55,000ft (16,764m).

Another improvement offered by the F.6 was its greater fuel capacity, which permitted Fighter Command squadrons from 1958 to undertake annual deployments to Malta and Cyprus for live firing practice over the less restricted Mediterranean ranges. The volume of air traffic in this region, both military and civil, also provided the opportunity for plenty of practice interceptions. As one squadron returned to the United Kingdom after completing an eastern Mediterranean deployment, it would at first land at the base of the next squadron to go out, so it could deliver the Hunter's outboard wing tanks, enabling the next unit's aircraft to make their ferry flights.

However, by this time it was clear the Hunter's day as a frontline interceptor was fast approaching the end and phasing out of the F.6, from premier Fighter Command units, commenced in 1960. Other reasons for this move were that several overseas air arms were acquiring supersonic fighters that outclassed the subsonic Hunters (despite their heavy armament and excellent manoeuvrability), while the RAF itself had the new supersonic Lightning interceptor entering service. The Hunter could out-turn F-100 Super Sabres based in Europe, but with its supersonic performance the latter could certainly attack or disengage as it wished.

Selected Hunter squadrons would re-equip with the FGA.9 as ground-attack specialists, and some were to be based in the UK, but 74 began acquiring Lightnings during 1960 and flew both these and Hunters until the latter finally departed in November that year. Nos 56 and 111 converted to Lightnings in 1961, while 66 disbanded in September 1960 and 65 Squadron during 1961. Of the survivors, 1 and 54 Squadrons came under the control of 38 Group, and 43 joined Near East Command based in Cyprus. Conversion from Hunters to Lightnings was undertaken by 19 Squadron from December 1962, but the last F.6 unit, 92, clung to its Hawker fighters until April 1963 when it too began to convert to the Lightning.

FGA.9

Tactical exercises had shown the F.6 to be a very good ground-support aeroplane and this led the way for the modified FGA.9 'mud-moving' version (the Sapphire-powered Hunter F.5s did not have full ground-attack strength factors). Full conversion to the FGA.9 by 1 and 54 Squadrons took much of 1961. As such they became the offensive element of 38 Group as the Fighter Command Short-Range Strike Wing, though they remained available for air defence

A Hawker Hunter on the strength of the ETPS at Farnborough was F.6 XF375. It is seen here in 1966, being flown by Flt Lt Graham Williams. (Key)

While serving with the ETPS in the early 1960s, T.7 WV253 sported a nose instrumentation boom. The aircraft is pictured at Dunsfold. (Adrian Balch)

F.6 XE601 was progressively brought up to FGA.9 standard, but never designated as such. It was used by the A&AEE at Boscombe Down for research (including biological warfare trials involving special tanks to spray water mist in simulated 'attacks') and with ETPS. This is it's later 'raspberry ripple' paint scheme. (Key)

Royal Navy GA.11 XE680 789/BY, of the HMS Goldcrest Training Flight (RNAS Brawdy) in December 1970. The scheme is Extra Dark Sea Grey over white, with Day-Glo panels on the spine, wingtips and nose. (Fred Motley)

duties if required. But the primary task was to develop close support and co-operation tactics with the Army, and there were frequent exercises for this, for example, Ringed Plover in May 1961, which involved co-operation over the North Yorkshire Moors. No 8 Squadron also reformed on the FGA.9 from January 1960.

To illustrate how training and practice programmes were arranged, in January 1963 seven of 54 Squadron's Hunters flew to Bahrain for a month's deployment as a Strike Wing mobility and rapid deployment trial. And May 1965 brought Exercise Easter Lightning in Scotland, where the wing provided support to an Army Brigade Group operating in counter-insurgency. Here the Hunters tried offensive operations against helicopters and defensive sorties in support of rotorcraft, but fast jets such as the Hunter were not really suited to such work. In June 1968, 54 Squadron sent most of its aircraft to northern Norway for Exercise Polar Express.

During the second half of the 1960s the training programme included Hunter detachments to armament practice camps at El Adem, Gibraltar or Gütersloh, West Germany, where the aircraft fired or dropped SNEB rockets or bombs and/or cannon. The Short-Range Strike Wing's final practice camp with the Hunter was to El Adem in March 1969; 54 Squadron then disbanded in September 1969, while in July that year No 1 began to re-equip with the Harrier.

For a short period in the 1970s two other UK-based units flew the FGA.9, 45 Squadron from August 1972 and 58 from August 1973. This was, however, a temporary measure to provide operational ground-attack experience for aircrew earmarked to fly the then new SEPECAT Jaguar, and this Hunter Wing was disbanded in July 1976. In September 1974, 229 OCU became the Strike Command Tactical Weapons Unit (TWU) comprising 63, 79 and 234 'Shadow' Squadrons. The TWU had some 60 Hunters on strength in four versions, the F.6 (but fitted with a Mk.9 rear fuselage along with its brake parachute), a hybrid F.6A with the FGA.9's stronger wings attached to an F.6 fuselage, T.7 two-seat trainers (see later) and the normal FGA.9s. A second interim TWU was formed in 1978.

RAF Hunter frontline service in general revolved around practice flying and training, both minor and major exercises for simulating real

WW664/699/LM was the T,8B prototype, but here wears 764 NAS markings at Lossiemouth on July 19, 1969. (the late Jim Halley, Air-Britain)

combat and war scenarios, and the interception of unidentified incoming aircraft – all to combat a threat which fortunately never reached the UK.

Senior Service

Bought for weapons training, the Royal Navy's single-seat Hunter was designated GA.11 and its two-seater the T.8. The GA.11 joined 738 (Advanced Training) Squadron in June 1962 and also equipped 764 Squadron. In December 1972 the surviving naval Hunters passed to the control of the Fleet Requirements and Air Direction Unit (FRADU), who's pilots were under contract to Airwork Services (and subsequently Flight Refuelling). FRADU's Hunters were used to make simulated attacks on warships as an aid to training radar and gun crews, and to calibrate their radars. Other tasks included, in 1982 prior to the departure of the Task Force that would repel Argentina's invasion of the Falklands, dissimilar air combat training against Sea Harriers. FRADU's Hunters were finally retired in May 1995.

2 TAF/RAF Germany

Deliveries of Hunter F.4s to the 2nd Tactical Air Force in Germany (from January 1959 RAF Germany) began in 1955, and its replacement by the F.6 began in early 1957. The large number of squadrons equipped with Hunters was organised into groups, wings and squadrons. Number 2 Group covered the airfields in northern West Germany and embraced 121 Wing at Gütersloh, Jever's 122 Wing, 124 Wing at Oldenburg and 125 Wing, Ahlhorn. Meanwhile 83 Group looked after the southern German airfields with 135 Wing at Brüggen and 138 Wing at Geilenkirchen.

The 1957 Defence White Paper disbanded many squadrons, while others switched to roles such as reconnaissance. Individually, 2 Squadron became the last unit to operate Hunters in Germany (until March 1971); 4 Squadron, the longest serving operational Hunter unit within the RAF as a whole, and 14 Squadron (the final F.6 operator), becoming the RAF's longest-serving Hunter day fighter unit.

Fortunately, the RAF Hawker Hunters in Germany were never called upon to take part in a real conflict, but the close proximity of the East German and Warsaw Pact borders meant their training necessarily had to be intense and realistic.

The Hunter F.4's main role here was again that of air defence. It was critical to have interceptors in a permanent state of readiness, so each airfield had a two-aircraft 'Battle Flight' ready for immediate response to scramble within five minutes of any violation of the Air Defence Identification Zone on the East German border. Two more Hunters would then replace those that had been scrambled, and each squadron would provide its base's Battle Flight faircraft for a week on a rotational basis.

XE530/A and XF417/B were Hunter F.6s serving with 26 Squadron out of Gütersloh when this slide was made in 1958-59. (John Merry)

This F.4, XE665 seen in 1955-56, was flown by the Wing Leader at Jever, Germany, and as such was adorned with the markings of the four resident squadrons: 4, 93, 98 and 118. (Brian Sharman via Roger Lindsay)

F.4 WW658/O of 98 Squadron in June 1956. This aircraft was never converted\ upgraded and was scrapped in 1964. (Key)

Hunter FR.10 XF458/W of 2 Squadron pictured in Germany, in the early 1960s.

Regular high-level practice interceptions were made against friendly aircraft under the control of ground-based radar stations. RAF types encountered included Meteors, Venoms and Canberras, while from other NATO air arms the Canadian Sabre was especially a fairly even match for the Hunter. There was also a monthly war exercise between 2 and 83 Groups, with as many as 60 aircraft flying at once. And twice a year each squadron would have live gun-firing on detachment to the Armament Practice Station at RAF Sylt, firing against banner targets towed over the North Sea.

The 1957 White Paper also brought changes to defence strategy, which for the F.6 brought more emphasis towards air-to-ground sorties with regular practice over the ranges at Meppen, Strohen and Nordhorn. T.7 trainers arrived in 1959 and examples were attached to each squadron, to Hunter Station Flights, the Armament Practice Station at Sylt and 402 Weapons Training Squadron. When the single-seat Hunters were retired, the T.7s continued with other frontline units in Germany operating types such as the Buccaneer. The trainer departed RAF Germany in 1984.

By the late 1950s, the arrival of new supersonic interceptors with advanced radars and guided missiles brought an end to the Hunter's air defence duties. The FGA.9 was never based in Germany, but deliveries of the FR.10 reconnaissance Hunter began in January 1961. The images collected at low level by the FR.10's cameras were used primarily by the British Army, and in large exercises this version proved superior to rival supersonic photo-recce types operated by other NATO air arms.

The RAF also had Hunters in the Middle and Far East, where they were either involved in armed conflict or at least a potential war situation. Their careers are described later.

The RAF's 4 Squadron flew Hunter F.4s and F.6s before converting to the recce FR.10 in late 1961, at Gütersloh in Germany. This example, XE580/D, carries a full complement of underwing tanks.

ROYAL AIR FORCE AND ROYAL NAVY HAWKER HUNTER UNITS

Due to the success of the Hunter, it was on strength with a great many British units throughout its career

(Note: Most operational RAF Squadrons had some T.7 two-seat trainers on strength)

F.1

43 Squadron – 8.54 to 8.56, Leuchars

54 Squadron – 2.55 to 9.55, Odiham

222 Squadron – 12.54 to 8.56, Leuchars

247 Squadron – 6.55 to 7.55, Odiham

43 and 222 Squadrons formed the Leuchars Wing, 54 and 247 the Odiham Wing.

Other Operators: 229 OCU (Chivenor), 233 OCU (Pembrey), Air Fighting Development Squadron (Wittering), Day Fighter Leaders' School (West Raynham), Fighter Weapons School (Leconfield, Driffield 10.57)

F.2

1 Squadron – two aircraft only 1955, Tangmere

257 Squadron – 9.54 to 3.57, Wattisham, Wymeswold (from 6.56), Wattisham (1.57)

263 Squadron – 2.55 to 8.56, Wattisham, Wymeswold (5.56)

257 and 263 formed the Wattisham Wing.

Other Operator: Air Fighting Development Squadron (Wittering)

F.4

3 Squadron – 6.56 to 6.57, Geilenkirchen, Germany

4 Squadron – 7.55 to 2.57, Jever, Germany

14 Squadron – 5.55 to 4.57, Oldenburg, Germany

20 Squadron – 11.55 to 6.57, Oldenburg

26 Squadron – 6.55 to 9.57, Oldenburg

43 Squadron – 3.56 to 12.56, Leuchars

54 Squadron – 8.55 to 1.57, Odiham

66 Squadron – 3.56 to 10.56, Linton-on-Ouse

67 Squadron – 1.56 to 5.57, Brüggen, Germany

71 Squadron – 4.56 to 5.57, Brüggen

74 Squadron – 3.57 to 1.58, Horsham St Faith

92 Squadron – 4.56 to 5.57, Linton-on-Ouse, Middleton St George (3.57)

93 Squadron – 1.56 to 4.57, Jever

98 Squadron – 4.55 to 7.57, Jever

111 Squadron – 6.55 to 11.56, North Weald

112 Squadron – 4.56 to 5.57, Brüggen

118 Squadron – 5.55 to 8.57, Jever

130 Squadron – 3.56 to 4.57, Brüggen

222 Squadron – 8.56 to 11.57, Leuchars

234 Squadron – 4.56 to 7.57, Geilenkirchen

245 Squadron – 3.57 to 6.57, Stradishall

247 Squadron – 5.55 to 3.57, Odiham

Other Operators: 229 OCU (Chivenor), Air Fighting Development Squadron (Wittering), Day Fighter Leaders' School (West Raynham), Fighter Weapons School (Leconfield, Driffield 10.57)

F.5

1 Squadron – 6.55 to 6.58, Tangmere

34 Squadron – 10.56 to 1.58, Tangmere

41 Squadron – 8.55 to 1.58, Biggin Hill

56 Squadron – 5.55 to 11.58, Waterbeach

208 Squadron – 1.58 to 2.58, Tangmere

257 Squadron – 7.55 to 3.57, Wattisham, Wymeswold (6.56), Wattisham (1.57)

263 Squadron – 4.55 to 8.56, Wattisham, Wymeswold (6.56)

1 and 34 formed the Tangmere Wing.

Other Operators: Air Fighting Development Squadron (Wittering)

F.6

1 Squadron – 7.58 to 6.60, Tangmere, Stradishall (7.58)

4 Squadron – 2.57 to 12.60, Jever

14 Squadron – 5.57 to 12.62, Oldenburg, Ahlhorn (9.57), Gütersloh (9.58)

19 Squadron – 10.56 to 11.62, Church Fenton, Leconfield (6.59)

20 Squadron – 5.57 to 12.60, Oldenburg, Ahlhorn (9.57), Gütersloh (9.58)

26 Squadron – 6.58 to 12.60, Ahlhorn, Gütersloh (9.58)

43 Squadron – 12.56 to 1960, Leuchars

54 Squadron – 1.57 to 3.60, Odiham, Stradishall (7.59)

56 Squadron – 11.58 to 1.61, Waterbeach, Wattisham (10.59)

63 Squadron – 11.56 to 10.58, Waterbeach

65 Squadron – 12.56 to 3.61, Duxford

66 Squadron – 10.56 to 9.60, Linton-on-Ouse, Acklington (2.57)

74 Squadron – 11.57 to 11.60, Horsham St. Faith, Coltishall (6.59)

92 Squadron – 2.57 to 4.63, Linton-on-Ouse, Middleton St George (3.57), Thornaby (9.57), Middleton St George (10.58), Leconfield (5.61)

93 Squadron – 3.57 to 12.60, Jever

111 Squadron – 11.56 to 4.61, North Weald, North Luffenham (2.58), Wattisham (6.58)

208 Squadron – 1.58 to 3.59, Tangmere, Nicosia (Cyprus 3.58)

247 Squadron – 3.57 to 12.57, Odiham

263 Squadron – 8.56 to 7.58, Wymeswold, Wattisham (1.57), Stradishall (8.57)

Other Operators 229 OCU (Chivenor), Air Fighting Development Squadron (Wittering, Coltishall from 9.69), Central Fighter Establishment (West Raynham), Central Flying School (Little Rissington), Day Fighter Leaders' School (West Raynham), Empire Test Pilots' School (ETPS at Farnborough), Fighter Weapons School (Leconfield, Driffield 10.57)

T.8 (Royal Navy)

700B NAS – 4.65 to 5.65, Lossiemouth

700Y NAS – 11.58 to 1.59, Yeovilton

700Z NAS – 5.61 to 12.62, Lossiemouth

736 NAS – 7.58 to 11.58, Lossiemouth

738 NAS – 6.62 to 5.70, Lossiemouth, Brawdy (1.64)

759 NAS – 7.63 to 12.69, Brawdy

764 NAS – 12.58 to 7.72, Lossiemouth

803 NAS – 5.60 to 7.60, Lossiemouth

899 NAS (T.8M) – 8.81 to 10.93, Yeovilton

FGA.9

1 Squadron – 3.60 to 7.69, Stradishall, Waterbeach (11.61), West Raynham (8.63)

4 Squadron – 9.69 to 3.70, West Raynham (on detachment)

8 Squadron – 1.60 to 12.67, Khormaksar

20 Squadron – 9.61 to 2.70, Tengah, Singapore

28 Squadron – 5.62 to 1.67, Kai Tak (Hong Kong)

43 Squadron – 1960 to 10.67, Leuchars, Nicosia (Cyprus, 6.61), Khormaksar (Aden, 3.63)

45 Squadron – 8.72 to 6.76, West Raynham, Wittering (9.72)

54 Squadron – 3.60 to 9.69, Stradishall, Waterbeach (11.61), West Raynham (8.63)

58 Squadron – 8.73 to 6.76, Wittering

208 Squadron – 3.60 to 9.71, Stradishall, Khormaksar (Aden 11.61), Muharraq (Bahrain 6.64)

Other Operators 229 OCU (Chivenor), 1 Tactical Weapons Unit (Brawdy)

FR.Mk.10

2 Squadron – 12.60 to 3.71, Jever, Gütersloh (9.61)

4 Squadron – 1.61 to 5.70, Jever, Gütersloh (9.61)

8 Squadron – 4.61 to 5.63 & 9.67 to 12.67, Khormaksar, Muharraq (9.67)

Other Operators 229 OCU (Chivenor)

1417 Flight 3.63 to 9.67 Khormaksar

GA.11 (Royal Navy)

738 NAS – 6.62 to 5.70, Lossiemouth, Brawdy (1.64)

764 NAS – 7.62 to 7.72, Lossiemouth

F.5 WN958 carrying bombs on the inner pylons and tanks on the outers. (Crown Copyright)

ALONE IN THE OFFICE

The first Hawker Hunter variants were the F.1, which was equipped with a Rolls-Royce Avon engine and the F.2, which had the same structure, armament and equipment but was powered by a R-R Sapphire unit.

The first production orders presented problems for Hawker Aircraft, at Kingston-upon-Thames, in finding sufficient manufacturing capacity, so to make room some Sea Hawk production was switched to Armstrong Whitworth. In fact, many 'Kingston' Hunters were completed at Langley (their major sub-assemblies came from Kingston) with initial flight trials at Dunsfold. Series aircraft were subsequently produced by Hawker Aircraft (Blackpool) Ltd and, for overseas, by Fokker (who undertook much of the licence manufacture in Holland), Aviolanda and de Schelde, and by SABCA and Avions Fairey in (and for) Belgium.

As noted, the one-off Mk.3 was prototype WB188, refitted with reheat as a trials aircraft. The fuel shortage afflicting the first two marks was addressed by the F.4 and F.5, both of which benefited from internal fuel inside bag-type tanks in the wings, the facility to carry a drop tank under each wing, plus 'Sabrina' blisters under the nose to collect used ammunition links. The F.4's maiden flight took place on October 20, 1954, and the F.5's just a day earlier. The latter retained the Mk.2's Sapphire Mk.101 engine,

The definitive gun muzzle layout was displayed by Hunter F.6 XE618 at the 1958 Farnborough airshow. The aircraft was converted to FGA.9 standard two years later. (Key)

although one example (serial WN955) performed flight trials with the up-rated 11,000lb (48.9kN) Sa.7.

A major advance was the P.1099 F.6 which introduced the more powerful Avon RA.28 and gave the Hunter improved performance overall. The prototype XF833, which incorporated the centre fuselage and nose from the abandoned P.1083 prototype WN470 (see later), first flew on January 22, 1954. The first production Mk.6 made its maiden flight on May 23, 1955, and later examples introduced a revised wing with four hardpoints and an extended leading edge with 'dogtooth'. Another change (and retrofitted to early production F.6s) was a fully-powered elevator to improve the Hunter's pitch response during flight at high mach numbers. Much later the F.6A appeared with a brake parachute and 230 gal (1,046 lit) drop tanks on the inboard pylons, specifically to permit sorties to be made from their RAF Brawdy base, where the available diversion airfields were some distance away.

The first Hawker Hunter F.1 was WT555. (All Tony Buttler unless stated)

In detail

The Hunter had a strong but conventional all-metal light alloy structure, with the frames numbered from 1 to 63. Its semi-monocoque fuselage was built in three sections – the nose housing the cockpit, armament pack and nosewheel, the centre section with the integral wing root stubs, the engine mountings and the intake ducts, and then the rear (detachable) fuselage with a hinged, hydraulically controlled flap airbrake (which could only be posed retracted or to full extension) curved to conform to the underside of the rear fuselage, an integral fin base, removable jetpipe and tail cone. The single-seat fighter had a sliding canopy that could be jettisoned, a pressurised and air-conditioned cockpit and a Martin-Baker ejection seat.

Gun armament for all single-seat versions comprised four 30mm Aden cannon in the nose (two left-hand, two right-hand) each with either 100 or 150 rounds, the latter giving a total firing time of seven seconds. These were housed in a self-contained quick-change pack fitted in the nose underside and which could be winch-lowered for re-arming and servicing (the gun barrels remained fixed to the airframe). The Adens were operated in conjunction with an automatic gun-ranging radar in the forward fuselage, its scanner in the extreme nose under a laminated plastic radome, and

In this pleasing study, groundcrew service a 65 Squadron Hunter F.6 at RAF Duxford in 1959. (Key)

Hunter underside views. The first shows F.4 WV319 in 1955, in clean condition (except for the airbrake) and with the original wing. The second has F.6 XK151 with wing extensions, 'Sabrina' link collectors and underwing pylons. (Crown Copyright)

a gyro gun sight. The engine was installed in the centre fuselage, and fed by air intakes in thickened wing-roots, while the exhaust went straight through to the end of the fuselage.

All flying surfaces were swept rearwards. The wing sported a symmetrical Hawker high-speed aerofoil section and was built around front and rear spars (with an undercarriage girder running diag-onally between) and covered by heavy-gauge skin panels. Hydraulically operated split flaps were positioned between the fully powered ailerons, and the fuselage and the ailerons had plain spring feel. The F.6's later leading-edge 'dogtooth' extensions provided greater chord on the outer wings, and were formed from short plate ribs with a heavy-gauge sheet wrapped around them and then riveted onto the original wing skin. The Mk.6 wings had a pair of stores pylons on each side to allow the aircraft to carry two 1,000lb (454kg) bombs, practice bomb carriers or four 100 gal (455 lit) finless asbestos plastic phenolic fuel tanks, or any combination thereof. And a total of 24 rocket projectiles could also be attached outboard of the fuel tanks, 12 carried per side.

The cantilever variable incidence tailplane was built as a single piece, it was mounted on the fin and again used Hawker's symmetrical high-speed aerofoil section. The surface was swept 41.9° at quarter chord and there was an anti-buffet bullet fairing at the rear junction of the fin and tail. Both tailplane and fin were skinned in light alloy, the elevators were fully powered and the electrically operated tailplane was also used for trimming. The fin employed closely spaced ribs connected to front and rear spars, it was swept 47.5° at the quarter-chord line and the rudder had an aerodynamic tab. Retractable Dowty tricycle-type undercarriage had the main wheels raising inward into the wing roots with the fully castoring nosewheel retracting forward into the fuselage (self-centring as it did so).

The F.6 had a larger tailpipe, while the version's automatic fuel system permitted the pilot to bang open the

The single-seat Hunter's gun pack, with barrels attached. (Key)

throttle, then close it and then open it again without risk of flame-out. In addition, the Avon 203 replaced the cartridge starter of earlier marks with an isopropyl-nitrate starting system, which allowed the engine to be rotated to self-sustaining rpm far more quickly, thereby allowing the Hunter to scramble in a much shorter time.

A study of Hunter rear fuselage detail provided by F.1 WT565.

Later versions

The F.6s converted to FGA.9 standard introduced a stronger wing, slightly more powerful Avon 207 engines, new mild steel 230 gal (1,046 lit) drop tanks on the inboard pylons, a 13ft 6in (4.11m) diameter tail parachute, and a bobweight in the pitch control circuit to provide more stick force for ground-attack manoeuvres. The first converted 'prototype' FGA..9, XG135, flew on July 3, 1959, and altogether

F.6s, 20 Squadron, Oldenburg, West Germany, 1959. The aircraft in the foreground, XJ680/A, was converted to FGA.9 standard the following year and delivered to 43 Squadron. (Key)

128 Mk.6s were upgraded as Mk.9s. In February 1968, FGA.9s received new Sperry gun sights, which provided air-to-air and air-to-ground modes for firing SNEB rockets, rocket projectiles or the guns.

During the mid-1950s a trial installation involved a forward-facing camera fitted in the nose of an F.4, and this brought forth a new requirement in 1957 for a modified Mk.6 to join RAF Germany, fitted with three F95 cameras, a braking parachute and 230 gal inboard drop tanks. Thus, the prototype fighter-reconnaissance FR.10 XF429, a converted F.6 airframe, first flew in modified form on November 7, 1959. In all, 33 F.6s were rebuilt to this configuration.

The next single-seat conversions comprised a batch of 40 surplus ex-RAF F.4s adapted for advanced weapons training for the Royal Navy. The resulting shore-based GA.11s had their guns removed, were fitted with an airfield arrester hook beneath the rear fuselage and had provision for rocket launchers on wing pylons. A small number subsequently had a Harley light fitted in the nose, to help with visual tracking when they operated as target aircraft…as such they were re-designated PR.11s. The first GA.11 began its trials programme in April 1962. Hunter production ended in the 1960s, but as related later, refurbishments would keep the manufacturer busy.

Testing

There is insufficient room to present detailed accounts of the assessment and approval testing of the various Hunter versions, but the following provides a flavour. In 1954 the Air Fighting Development Unit, part of the Central Fighter Establishment (CFE), performed tactical trials with Mk.1 and 2 aircraft for the interception of enemy bombers. From an aerobatic standpoint the Hunter F.1 was found to be light and responsive to the controls, and all standard aerobatic manoeuvres could be executed with ease, although a considerable amount of height could be gained or lost during manoeuvres in the looping plane.

The handsome Chinthe badge and green/yellow checkers mark this Hunter, WN915/T, as an F.2 of 257 Squadron, which flew the type from 1954-57. (Key)

The FR.10 prototype was XF429. Note the nose camera windows to the side and extreme front. (Key)

The sleek lines of the Hawker Hunter are shown to great effect in this splendid manufacturer's view of GA.11 WV380 taken, it is thought, prior to delivery to the Royal Navy. The Mk.11 had the extended wing leading edges.

They were, however, not well suited to the low-level role because of the small amount of fuel carried. The equivalent testing of Mks.4 and 5 in July 1955, with their extra fuel, found that the increased weight had produced a slightly detrimental effect on the performance and they were inferior to the F.1 and F.2 in fighter v fighter combat, but this was considered acceptable in view of the extended range and endurance. However, both marks were still not really ideal for low-level work.

Tactical trials with the F.6 were made in October 1956 and the greater all-up weight and increased thrust had given a shorter take-off run, a reduced time to height, slight increase in maximum level speed, and faster acceleration/deceleration, but a penalty was that increased fuel consumption reduced the radius of action and ferry range. The F.6 could intercept a bomber flying at Mach 0.85 at 45,000ft (13,716m) and the improved time to height enabled interceptions to be made 24 miles (39km) further out over the Mks.4/5. Times to 40,000ft (12,192m) were:

F.1 - 7 mins 48 secs, F.2 - 6 mins 20 secs, F.4 - 8 mins 35 secs, F.5 - 7 mins 40 secs and F.6 - 6 minutes.

A Ministry document from March 1956 gave the equivalent maximum speeds for each of these marks at 45,000ft (13,716m) as 524 kts (971km/h), 529 kts (980km/h), 521 kts (965km/h), 527 kts (977km/h) and 532 kts (986km/h).

The F.6 with the 'electric flying tail' (fully powered elevator) and the parallel extended leading edges gave a noticeably more pleasant take-off and lighter stick forces. Its capability in the high-altitude interceptor role was not affected by the addition of the leading-edge extensions, but these markedly reduced the tendency for pitch-up prevalent in earlier versions – and provided more manoeuvrability for fighter v fighter combat at medium and low altitudes. The electric tail also provided a distinct improvement in longitudinal control at high Mach numbers. CFE added that the F.6 was a very satisfactory and stable rocket-firing platform. This trait, coupled with external fuel tanks, handling characteristics, speed and gun/rocket armament made the mark an excellent air support weapon, and would result in the FGA.9. The initial CA Release for the Mk.6 cleared it for service use in the interceptor role by day only, in temperate climates with a maximum take-off and flying weight of 17,500lb (7,938kg) and a maximum permissible speed (strength limitation) of 620kts (1,149km/h) Indicated Air Speed, except when firing the guns. Within this speed limit there was no barrier regarding Mach number.

Hunter FGA.9 XG207/R of 45 Squadron 'Flying Camels' about to land. The unit received its Hunters on reformation at RAF West Raynham in 1972, but it moved to Wittering almost immediately in its duties as a ground-attack training outfit, until it disbanded in 1976.

COMPLETE HAWKER HUNTER PRODUCTION LIST

Hunter T.8C XF357/637/LM, of 738 NAS, Lossiemouth, in 1962. (Key)

Built in UK for British service

Hawker P.1081 Research Aircraft (converted from P.1052).

VX279 (1 - built at Kingston)

Hawker P.1067 Prototypes

WB188, WB195, WB202 (3 all built at Kingston)

Hawker P.1083 Prototype

WN470 (1 – Kingston – not completed)

Hawker P.1099 (F.6 Prototype)

XF833 (1 from Kingston)

Hawker P.1101 Two-Seat Prototypes

XJ615, XJ627 (2 both Kingston)

Hunter F.1

WT555-WT595, WT611-WT660, WT679-WT700 (113 all Kingston); WW599-WW610, WW632-WW645 (26 all built at Blackpool)

F.2

WN888-WN921, WN943-WN953 (45 all built by Armstrong Whitworth at Coventry)

F.3

WB188 (1 prototype modified for research and speed record at Kingston)

F.4

WT701-WT723, WT734-WT769, WT771-WT780, WT795-WT811, WV253-WV281, WV314-WV334, WV363-WV412, WW589-WW591 (189 all Kingston – WT770 direct to Sweden); WW646-WW665, XE657-XE689, XE702-XE718, XF289-XF324, XF357-XF370, XF932-XF953, XF967-XF999, XG341 and XG342 (177 all Blackpool)

F.5

WN954-WN992, WP101-WP150 and WP179-WP194 (105 all Coventry)

F.6

WW592-WW598, XE526-XE561, XE579-XE628, XE643-XE656, XG127-XG137 (118 all Kingston); XG150-XG168 (19 all Armstrong Whitworth, Baginton, Coventry); XG169-XG172, XG185-XG211, XG225-XG239, XG251-XG274, XG289-XG298, XJ632-XJ646, XJ673-XJ695, XJ712-XJ718, XK136-XK176, XK213-XK224 (178 all Kingston – XK157-XK176, XK213-XK224 = 32 completed as Mk.56 for India as BA201-BA232); XF373-XF389, XF414-XF463, XF495-XF527 (100 all Armstrong Whitworth Coventry)

T.7

XL563-XL579, XL583, XL586, XL587, XL591-XL597, XL600, XL601, XL605, XL609-XL623 (45 all Kingston)

T.8

XL580-XL582, XL584, XL585, XL598, XL599, XL602-XL604 (10 all Kingston)

Built in UK for overseas service

Denmark

F.51 (based on F.4)

E-401 to E-430 (30 all Kingston)

T.7

ET-271, ET-272 (2 both Kingston)

India

F.56 (based on F.6)

BA201-BA232, BA249-BA360 (160 of which 145 new build by Kingston)

BA233-BA248 ex-RAF machines, though BA239 (ex-XE600) rejected and new BA239 built by Hawker

T.66

BS361-BS376, BS485-BS490 (22 all Kingston)

Jordan

T.66B (based on P.1101 trainer)

714 (1 from Kingston)

Netherlands

T.7

N-301 to N-320 (20 all Kingston)

Sweden

F.50 (based on F.4 and in Sweden designated J 34)

34001-34024, (24 all Kingston – ex-WT770 became 34001); 34025-34120 (96 all Blackpool)

Switzerland

F.58 (based on F.6)

J-4013 to J-4100 (88 all Kingston – J-4001 to J-4012 ex-RAF machines sold unused)

Built Overseas Under License

Belgium

F.4

ID-1 to ID-64, ID-101 to ID-148 (112 all built by Avions Fairey/SABCA)

F.6

IF-1 to IF-144 (144 all built by Avions Fairey/SABCA)

Netherlands

F.4

N-101 to N-196 (96 all built by Fokker/Aviolanda)

F.6

N-201 to N-293 (93 all Fokker/Aviolanda)

Grand total new-build Hunter: 1,972

(Overseas conversions are detailed under their respective chapters.)

Rockets are salvoed by a 1 Squadron FGA.9 at Cowden North range, East Yorkshire, 1964. (Key)

FOR INSTRUCTIONAL PU

Hawker's two-seater G-APUX was demonstrated at Farnborough in 1960, with large 350 gal (1,591 lit) external ferry tanks. These were produced by inserting two 3ft (0.91m) sections into standard 230 gal (1,046 lit) tanks. Each had a lateral bracing strut and was stressed to 7g for ground-attack sorties. Note the gun and link collector arrangement. (Hawker Aircraft)

The Hunter fighter's flying qualities were so good that it was no surprise Hawker would produce a two-seat version.

Although the trainer variants did not win the orders one might have expected from UK air arms, they proved popular overseas. In addition, although the number of new-build airframes was quite small, the relatively simple replacement of the original cockpits with the two-seat form enabled the manufacturer to modify many obsolescent and redundant Mk.4 and Mk.6 airframes, which might otherwise have been discarded.

Hawker P.1101

Design studies for Hunter two-seater trainers began in 1953 under Hawker project number P.1101, and official specification T.157D was raised to cover orders for the RAF. It was decided the single-seat airframe should remain unaltered rearwards of the front transport joint bulkhead, just forward of the wing-root intakes (ie identical to the Mk.4). The Hunter's modular construction made fitting a new nose reasonably easy and both tandem and side-by-side seating were considered, the latter because it was favoured for instrument flying and weapons training, while tandem seats proved best for advanced flying instruction. The tandem layout's weakness was that the necessary longer forward fuselage would require more vertical tail area, which in turn would increase the load on the rear fuselage, and so side-by-side was the choice.

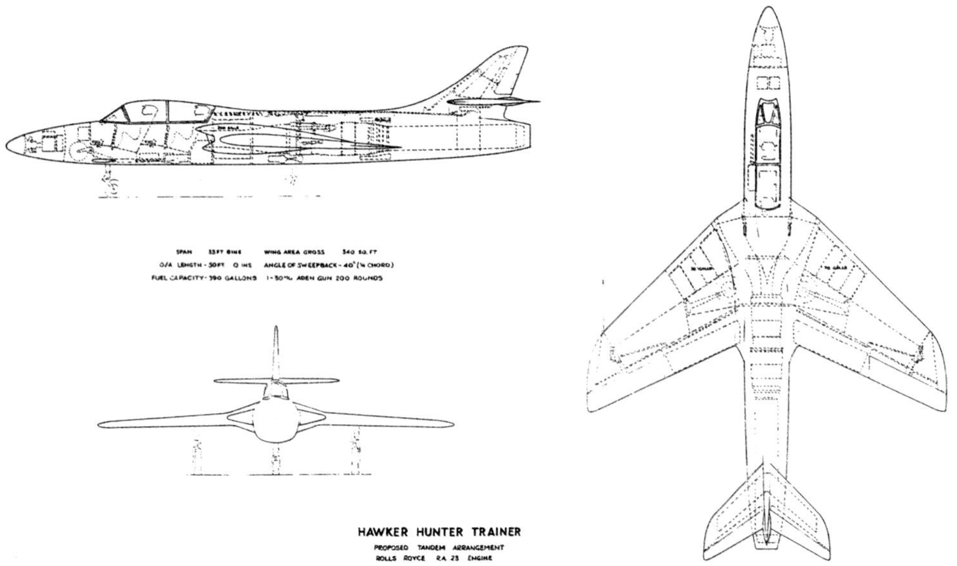

Drawings were prepared for a tandem-format two-seat Hunter. This Hawker P.1101 three-view for an aircraft with an RA.23 Avon engine does not carry a date. It had a span of 35ft 8in (10.87m), overall length 50ft (15.24m) and wing area 340sq ft (31.62m²). It carried one 30mm Aden in the port side forward fuselage, and 390 gal (1,773 lit) of fuel. (Hawker Aircraft)

The first of two prototypes, XJ615, made its first flight on July 8, 1955,

RPOSES

A 1959 study of a T.7 cockpit. Note the two head-up displays. (Hawker Aircraft)

piloted by Neville Duke. In the air, the original prototype cockpit shape with its small fore-and-aft fairing produced unacceptable turbulence and buffeting, and much noise over the canopy. An extended dorsal fairing only partly overcame these flaws, and the P.1101's handling characteristics were not perfect either. In early 1956 a wider and rather more bulbous fairing was introduced, which proved completely successful. There was some worry that this much fatter body, positioned ahead of the wing-root air intakes, might affect the engine and possibly cause flame-outs under certain conditions, but this proved not to be the case.

The new pressurised two-seat, side-by-side cockpit housed two lightweight Martin-Baker ejection seats and two standard fighter-type control columns. The cockpit also had two gun sights but most of the equipment was concentrated in the left (pupil's) seat to essentially re-create a single-seat cockpit (with the single-seater's starboard console in the centre panel). On the right side the instructor had just a gun sight, altimeter, horizon, airspeed indicator and machmeter. Initially, XJ615 carried two 30mm Aden cannon in fixed ventral installations – quite different to the single-seater's replaceable four-cannon pack – but the port side weapon was removed later, and a blast deflector introduced to eliminate pitch and yaw when firing the starboard cannon. The new large canopy was heavy, and it was critical to ensure pilots did not get their arms in the way when it was closing. The solution was a horn that sounded continuously while the hood lowered, and it stopped only when the canopy was locked (signified by a small green light).

Despite the more bulbous forward fuselage, the trainer's compressibility drag-rise was delayed over the single seater; this balanced the larger surface area and so the F.4 and trainer showed no measurable difference in maximum level speed. XJ615 was powered by an F.4 standard 100-series Avon, and in April 1956 it began trials with a 10ft 6in (3.20m) diameter tail parachute

The first P.1101 prototype XJ615, pictured before a brake chute had been installed. A dark panel in front of the windscreen shows the limit of a temporary Perspex shield used to provide a smooth airflow over the hood. (Hawker Aircraft)

One of the T.8M conversions with Sea Harrier radar was serialled XL603. It sports 899 NAS's winged fist motif. (Key)

The RAE's T.12 wore a vivid green and white colour scheme. This mid-1960s view shows the distinctive bulge on top of its nose to cover the camera fitting. A P.1127 V/STOL prototype sits in the distance, behind the nosewheel.

to provide braking and reduce the landing run. This was housed in a fairing above the jet pipe, with the chute being anchored to the airframe.

The second two-seat prototype, XJ627, was quite different because it had a 9,950lb (44.22kN) Avon 200-series engine (making it an equivalent to the F.6) and the definitive forward fuselage from the start. Produced with the export market in mind, it first flew on November 17, 1956 and with the more powerful Avon, and delayed compressibility, it was marginally faster than the F.6. Hunter XJ627 had the drag parachute fairing, saw-tooth leading-edge extensions and a much more powerful horizontal tail control through the introduction of a fully powered elevator. The range of incidence for the tailplane was +31° to -2°. In essence this was an 'all-flying' tail and the aircraft's response at high Mach numbers, or during pronounced manoeuvring, was excellent. Coupled with the more powerful engine this made for a superior aircraft over the initial T.7/T.8 family.

Hawker Aircraft also acquired its own private two-seater, which served as a valuable demonstration/development airframe. This Hunter carried the civil registration G-APUX and was designated Mk.66A. It was rebuilt using repaired component sections from two crashed Belgian F.6s, which were joined to a standard Indian Air Force Mk.66 cockpit that had previously been displayed at a Farnborough Show. It also sported two guns and an oversized braking parachute and made its maiden flight in this condition on August 12, 1959. Hawker Chief Test Pilot 'Bill' Bedford, Neville Duke's successor, flew G-APUX at Farnborough in 1959 and 1960, and during his displays he used smoke (created by injecting diesel oil into the exhaust) to demonstrate 12-turn erect spins starting from altitudes of approximately 15,000ft (4,572m). Recovery from a spin was straightforward, by centralising the control column against a white mark on the instrument panel. After having been test-flown by several air forces, in the process proving a major contribution to winning new orders (for example in 1959 it was leased to the Swiss Air Force), G-APUX was in 1966 converted to a T.72 with the serial J-718 for the Chilean Air Force. However, no T.66 variants joined British air arms, since sufficient F.4s were available for conversion to T.7/T.8 standard.

Royal Navy T.8 XF322 was converted from an F.4 and is seen here in the 1960s, as 962/HF of the Hal Far Test Flight, Malta. (Air-Britain)

T.7

The RAF's order for two-seat Hunters, designated T.7s, covered 55 new-build airframes, but in due course ten of these were switched to a Royal Navy T.8 order. A supplementary acquisition meant another 28 F.4s were converted to Mk.7 standard, which brought the RAF compliment to 73. The Mk.7 equated to late-production F.4s, so the wing had provision for two outboard pylons and rocket pods plus eight sets of 3in (76.2mm) rocket projectiles. The first production machine was serial XL563, which first became airborne on October 11, 1957.

Hawker had hoped the RAF would

In early 1960 T.62 '681', ex-F.4 WT706, became the only two-seater acquired by Peru. The photo was taken at Hawker in autumn 1959 and the aircraft was delivered by sea. (Hawker Aircraft)

select the T.7 as its new advanced trainer to replace the de Havilland Vampire, but the small and cheaper Folland Gnat was bought instead and so the T.7s were used for tactical weapons instruction, and to provide advanced flying training specifically for 'tall' students and for overseas pilots on attachment to the RAF. The first production deliveries, in August 1958, went to 229 Operational Conversion Unit at Chivenor and frontline Hunter squadrons usually had one each. When the fighter was retired, surplus T.7s joined 4 Flying Training School at Valley. Four more were used for trials and one, XL574, was subsequently fatigue-tested to destruction. Three more flew with the Air Fighting Development School. A later sub-type was the T.7A, which was fitted with an Integrated Flight Instrumentation System (IFIS) to train and convert pilots to fly the English Electric Lightning interceptor, and Blackburn Buccaneer strike aircraft.

T.8

The ten two-seat trainers diverted to the Royal Navy were designated T.8 and were supplemented by another 18 F.4 conversions. These were to be used to train de Havilland Sea Vixen and Supermarine Scimitar fighter pilots, and the main difference from the T.7 was the fitting of an arrestor hook. However, the T.8 was not stressed for carrier-capability and the hook was to be employed for practice landings on normal airfields. Rebuilt F.4 WW664 served as the T.8 prototype and first flew in this form on March 3, 1958. The first new-build T.8 was XL580, first flown on May 30, 1958, and deliveries began during the summer.

Later, to train Buccaneer pilots, four examples were modified as T.8Bs with a TACAN radio-navigation system and IFIS (both guns and ranging radar were removed). Eleven more were converted to T.8Cs with TACAN and some of these carried a Harley light in their noses. From 1979 there was the T.8M fitted with the Sea Harrier fighter's Blue Fox radar in a pointed nose. Three examples were upgraded as T.8Ms for training Sea Harrier pilots.

A beautiful study of WV363, a T.8 from 764 NAS, carrying rockets and practice bombs. (Key)

This RAF T.7 was on strength with 54 Squadron, judging by that unit's smart blue and yellow marking on the nose. (Chris Goss)

T.12

Finally, from the British perspective, there was the one-off T.12 serial XE531. This was a converted former F.6/FGA.9 with an Avon 203 and was delivered as a two-seater in February 1963. It carried no guns and was earmarked for service with RAE Farnborough and Bedford. In its nose was a trial installation of a large vertical survey camera, together with head-up displays (HUDs) in the cockpit to

The Royal Netherlands Air Force was the only overseas air arm to operate all-new-build two-seat Hunters, rather than converted airframes. This view shows 'N-304', which was first flown on June 24, 1958, by Hawker test pilot Frank Bullen. (Key)

enable its pilots to perform trials for the forthcoming BAC TSR.2 strike aircraft. The latter's need to approach a target at low level beneath enemy radar, using terrain-following gear, had helped in the development of a head-up display, which was then very advanced equipment. On this Hunter, the camera fitting was visible in the form of a distinctive bulge on top of its nose to accommodate the equipment.

Extensive trials ensured more than 100 hours' flying was recorded by early September 1964, which proved the validity and effectiveness of the basic principle. At one point it seemed likely that further examples might be converted to a similar standard, to enable the Mk.12 to become a TSR.2 instrument trainer, but in 1965 the strike aircraft was cancelled and so XE531 remained the sole example. Nevertheless, these trials resulted in a useful accumulation of experience in advanced instrumentation. Afterwards RAE used XE531 for more research, for example with a fly-by-wire flight control system. It eventually lost the distinctive nose bulge, but the aircraft was lost in an accident in March 1982. This was the only UK-based two-seat Hunter with the powerful Avon Mk.203/207 powerplant.

Overseas Orders

A multitude of nations bought two-seat Hunters, the 200-series especially serving either as a trainer or tactical aircraft. Some two-seat overseas orders were new-build airframes and are highlighted in this book's production list, but the deliveries detailed below were all conversions from retired F.4s or F.6s or, in some cases, acquired second-hand from other air arms.

Exports with the Avon 100-series were Abu Dhabi (2 x T.77s, serials 711 and 712 – ex Danish T.7s), Denmark (2 x T.53, serials ET-273 and ET-274 to supplement new-build), Kenya (2 x T.81, 801 and 802), Peru (1 x T.62 serial 681), Qatar (1 x T.79, QA-13, ex-Dutch), Saudi Arabia (2 x T.7, 70/616 and 70/617, ex-RAF), Singapore (4 x T.75, 500, 504, 514 and 516, and 5 x T.75A, 528, 532, 536, 540 and 544), Somalia (1 x T.77, CC-711 ex-Dutch) and Switzerland (8 x T.68, which had provision for carrying Sidewinder air-to-air missiles, J-4201 to J-4208).

India's two-seaters were based on the second P.1101, XJ627, with the more powerful engine and they had a second 30mm gun. This was the first order for the later trainer version and the 200-series Avon allowed higher take-off weights for India's hotter temperatures. There were 22 new-build T.66s plus 12 T.66Ds with two 1,045 lit (230 gal) drop tanks (serials S570 to S581) and 5 T.66Es with different avionics (S1389 to S1393). Other two-seaters fitted with the 200-series Avon went to Chile (7 x T.72, serials J-718 - J-723 plus J-736), Iraq (5 x T.69, 567-569, 626 and 627), Jordan (1 x new build plus 3 x T.66B conversions, 714, 716, 718 and 722), Kuwait (5 x T.67, 210, 211 and 218-220), Lebanon (3 x T.66C, L-280 to L-282) and Oman (3 x T.66B and 2 x T.67, 800-804).

Like the single-seaters, the Hunter two-seat versions were all rather short of internal fuel, so had to carry external tanks to achieve a satisfactory range. But in service they proved hugely successful and in general had long service lives.

Singapore Air Force T.75 '500' at RAF Brawdy, Wales on June 28, 1976. (Key)

▼ Hunter T.7, XL616/D, 208 Squadron RAF, 1993. Overall matt black.

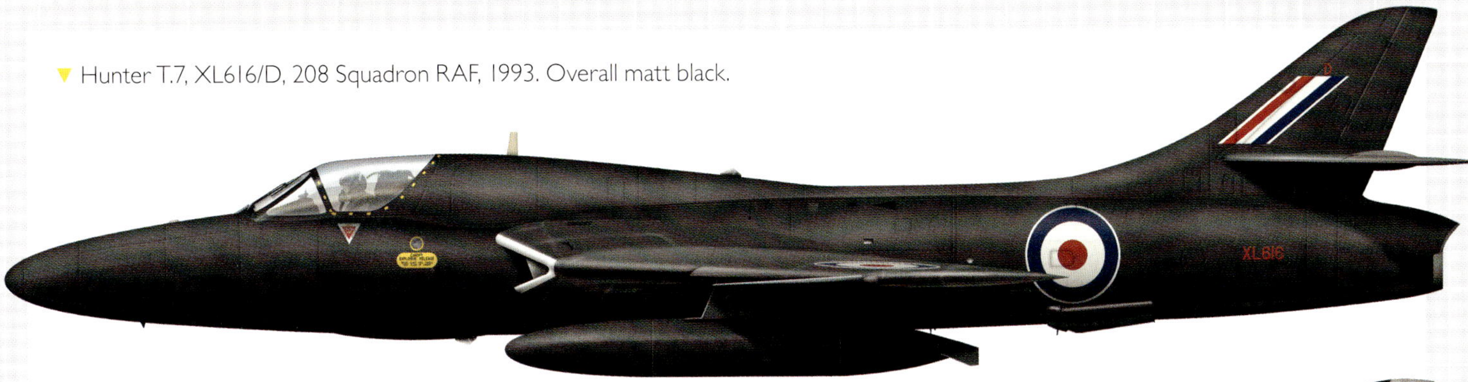

▼ Hunter T.8, XE664/708/LM. 764 NAS, Lossiemouth, 1962. High Speed Silver with yellow trainer bands.

▼ Hunter T.8C, XE665, Fleet Requirements and Air Direction Unit, Yeovilton, on loan to 208 Squadron RAF, Honington, September 1980. Light Aircraft Grey with Signal Red high-visibility panels.

▼ Hunter T.7, XL619/77, 45 Squadron RAF, Wittering, 1974. Dark Green, Dark Sea Grey and Light Aircraft Grey.

▼ Hunter T.8M, XL603/724, 899 NAS, Yeovilton, July 1992. Overall Dark Sea Grey.

(Andy Hay/www.flyingart.co.uk)

EXPANDING THE ENV

XF310, with two dummy Fairey Fireflash missiles and a nose-mounted ranging radar, was captured in this publicity photo prior to or during the 1956 Farnborough show. Note the absence of roundels and markings, due to the RAF not wanting any insignia shown because it still had not endorsed the weapon. (Tony Buttler)

Unlike other British aircraft such as the Gloster Meteor fighter and English Electric Canberra bomber (both of which had two engines and were well suited as engine test beds, and trials airframes for new avionics such as radars), the Hunter was not used extensively for general research programmes.

However, a number of single-seat airframes were adapted for experimental use, but in many cases purely for possible future developments of the basic airframe. The listing that follows is not exhaustive. Much more detail is available in the author's book The Design and Development of the Hawker Hunter (History Press 2014).

Airframe

To begin with, one further change from the standard design was considered by Hawker.

In February 1953, American sources

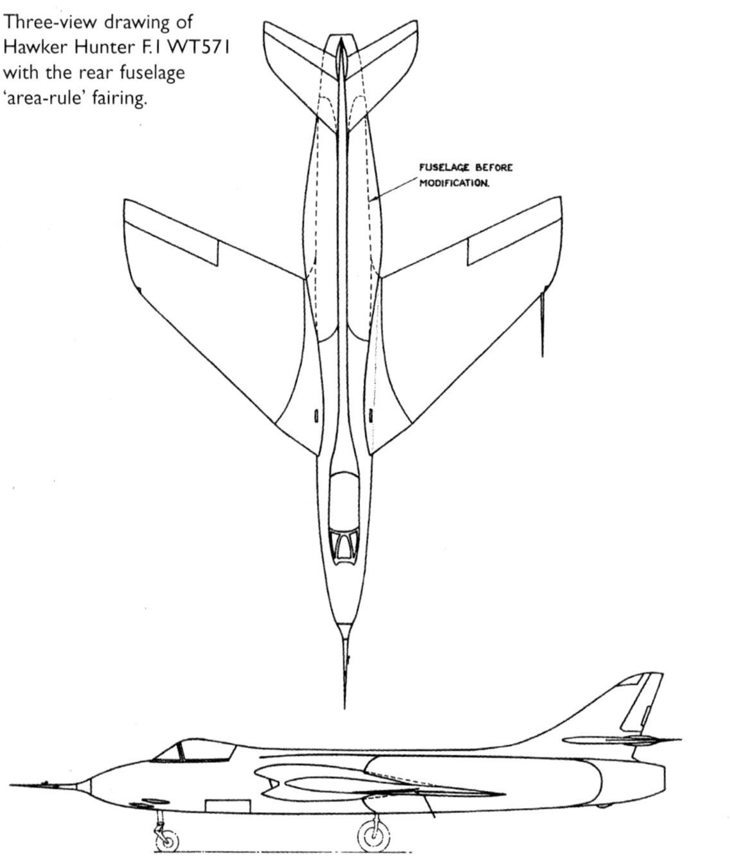

Three-view drawing of Hawker Hunter F.1 WT571 with the rear fuselage 'area-rule' fairing.

A close up of XG131's tip tank fitting taken on September 7, 1956. The aircraft was mounted on jacks during the show. (Phil Butler)

quoted designer Sydney Camm as favouring external tanks 'snuggled up under the wings' on the Hunter, as opposed to wing tip tanks. Tip tanks had been assessed but appear to have been rejected, and in that November's *Flight* magazine noted: "reports of a Hunter flying with slipper tanks mounted on the undersides of the wings are incorrect; such a development has not yet been flown". Then in September 1956, Hunter F.6 XG131 appeared at Farnborough (static only) with permanently attached, partly underslung metal tip tanks of 85 gal (386 lit) capacity, and which had finely faired sleeves over the normal wing tips; these tanks had navigation lights in their noses. In other respects, XG131 was a standard F.6 and it first flew in this form on August 16, 1956, but unacceptable buffet was encountered (in fact possibly the highest level of buffet ever experienced by any Hunter). The aircraft apparently flew appallingly, this new arrangement ruining the Hunter's aerodynamics particularly at high incidence. Underwing tanks proved far better, and so no further work was undertaken on this project, which never received any Ministry backing. Hunter XG131 was subsequently restored to standard F.6 configuration.

As a brief illustration of the sort of research that was ongoing, especially during the mid-1950s, in July 1957 *Flight* magazine reported that three Hunters were with the Royal Aircraft Establishment (RAE) at Bedford. One had been mounted on a simple rig to determine moments-of-inertia in pitch, accurate measurements of the natural period of oscillation, together with data on the aircraft's weight and centre-of-gravity positions, yielding the required information. A second had been used to measure loads on the complete tailplane during in-flight manoeuvres, electrical strain-

An entirely new experimental 'interceptor and ground-attack development' Hunter variant appeared in the static park at Farnborough, in 1956; XG131 fitted with tip tanks. This rare Hawker photo taken on October 5 that year is one of the few to show it flying in this form. (Hawker Aircraft)

Hunter WT656 with the Attinello flaps lowered. This aircraft also sported a nose probe. (Barry Jones)

gauges recording the surface strain on the tailplane attachment fittings. A third measure was then employed to reduce transonic drag by introducing the 'area-rule' concept. Area-rule was best applied to the design of a new aeroplane right at the start, but it was felt that the drag of existing types could also be reduced by adding suitable fairings.

In 1955, F.1 WT571 had bulbous fairings attached to its rear fuselage, though in fact because of its shape the Hunter fuselage could never be truly area-ruled. After modification, WT571 returned to RAE Farnborough in early July 1955 to begin its flying programme, which lasted until October. The results indicated that just small increases in transonic performance had been achieved, though there was no increase in subsonic drag and a negligible change to WT571's handling characteristics. When flying in formation with another Hunter, the rear fairing had improved the maximum level-speed performance by about Mach 0.01 to 0.015. The fairing was not fitted to any other Hunter airframe and *Flight* reported that WT571 was later used to: "develop a technique of photographing shockwaves in flight, using direct sunlight as the illuminating source".

From June to September 1955, RAE used another F.1, WT656, to assess Attinello blown flaps fitted in place of the Hunter's normal split trailing-edge flaps. This form of boundary layer control would enable the wing to develop increased lift at low airspeeds, primarily to reduce take-off and landing speeds/distances.

Boundary layer control took the form of supersonic blowing over the special Attinello plain flaps, air being bled from the Avon compressor and ducted to the wings, where it was ejected at supersonic speed through a slot 1.52mm wide, which extended over the flap's entire span. There was also a long nose pitot with a swivelling head to serve as the air speed indicator.

The flight test programme included general handling, measured take-offs, blown landings and stalls, and the results showed a reduction in stalling speed of between 1-10 kts (1.9-18.5km/h), dependant on flap angle and engine rpm. However, this blown flap system for the Hunter had produced several new problems, including a strong nose-down pitch which, at low speeds, reduced the effectiveness of the elevator and tailplane. With blow operating there was also a reduction in engine thrust from 7,600lb to 6,700lb, restricting engine speeds on the approach. From the Hunter perspective, the only practical benefit of this system appeared to be the nose-down attitude, which improved the pilot's forward and downward view. From December 1957, WT656 was used for barrier trials and then from December 1959 was employed in noise tests at the Larkhill rocket-firing site.

Powerplants

In 1955, F.5 WN955 was fitted with an 11,000lb (48.9kN) thrust Sapphire Sa.7 200-series engine as a 'Mk.6 standby', which it is assumed was

WT571 pictured at Farnborough, with the fairing attached to each side of its rear fuselage. (Barry Jones)

The thrust reverser trials Hunter XF833 poses for publicity photos at the 1956 Farnborough show.

insurance against possible failure of the Avon 200 series F.6 development programme. The first flight with the Sa.7 installed was made on February 9, 1956. WN955 was painted silver and carried Class B mark 'G-1-2', but no photo has ever been found of the aircraft in Sa.7 configuration. From mid-July 1959 this Hunter was used by RAE's Radio Department for ground trials, which included running the engine to enable infra-red measurements.

Possibly the most important trial concerning Hunter powerplants was the fitting of a Rolls-Royce thrust reverser to F.6 prototype XF833. This formed part of a general research programme for the Rolls-Royce Conway engine, which was to be fitted to forthcoming transatlantic airliners. When reverse thrust was selected, a pair of hemispherical eyelid shutters inside the Hunter's end fuselage would close, so that all of the RA.28's efflux was ejected through new lateral rectangular outlet grille exits in the rear fuselage sides, with multiple cascade vanes deflecting the exhaust outwards and forwards. XF833 was converted in mid-1956, and the work involved minimal external modification to airframe or engine. Trials began in November 1956 and 308 landings had been recorded by April 1958. It was established that the landing roll distance with no reverse thrust and full braking was 2,520ft (768m), while the average with thrust reversing was an average of 919ft (280m) less.

XF833's reverse-thrust grille. For the September 1956 Farnborough, the Hunter had a smoke generator in the tailpipe to show the direction of gas flow when landing.

What is apparently the first photo to be released to the press of the Fireflash-armed Hunter. The date is given as August 29, 1956, although the aircraft appears to have its later Mk.10 nose.

Side-angle view of XF310 after RAF roundels had been applied. Fireflash had originally been codenamed Blue Sky. (Tony Buttler)

Guided weapons

In 1956 Hunter F.4 XF310 was converted to carry two Fairey Fireflash beam-riding air-to-air missiles under its wings, suspended from the inner pylons on a spigot at the front, and a ball and socket bearer well aft under the wing. Beam-riding meant the pilot could 'fly' the weapon down a radio beam emitted by and aimed at the target by the launch aircraft. XF310's nose was extended and had an enlarged black dielectric nose cap radome to accommodate the beam-laying Mk.2 ranging radar. The four-gun armament stayed, but the camera port just aft of the radome was made deeper and longer, and normal pitot heads were mounted at both wing tips. In this form, XF310 first flew on July 18, 1956, and it displayed satisfactory handling characteristics.

For the 1956 Farnborough Show, XF310 carried no national markings and was painted blue underneath, with the two missiles adorned with what was described as 'a rather lurid colour'. Successful firing trials were completed in January 1957, and by September 1957's Farnborough, the dielectric nose cap had been replaced by an FR.10 nose with a vertical glass window, but no camera. Fireflash was not adopted by the RAF and XF310 was later converted to a T.7.

A much larger programme was an attempt to give the Hunter the capability to carry the de Havilland Firestreak infrared-homing air-to-air missile, which until 1957 was codenamed Blue Jay. Work began in 1953, but official Ministry support was cancelled in May 1956; however, Hawker elected to continue this effort as a private venture. With more engine thrust, the Firestreak radar/missile combination could be fitted to the standard subsonic Hunter without any loss of performance, and this would increase the fighter's interception capabilities, particularly at night. The new version was called the Hawker P.1109 and was a modified F.6 with (as planned) an 11,250lb (50.0kN) thrust Avon RA.24 (this in fact was never installed), a more pointed nose for an AI.Mk.20 air interception radar (codenamed Green Willow) and just two guns to reduce the nose weight. Otherwise the aircraft was largely a standard Mk.6 but it did not have the extended wing leading edges, and overall it was approximately 3ft (0.91m) longer. There was no intention to clear the P.1109 as a weapon system.

Three F.6s were selected for the trials, WW594, WW598 and XF378, although just XF378 received the complete conversion with radar, missiles and wing pylons to carry the

Close-up of one of XF310's Fireflash missiles (a dummy) at Farnborough in 1957. The store was launched towards its targets by booster rockets. (Key)

At one stage, Sapphire engine prototype WB202 had four dummy Firestreak air-to-air missiles loaded under the wings. Flight trials took place in May-June 1954, but were not connected with the later P.1109 programme. (Tony Buttler)

latter. The first two were aerodynamic test beds – they had AI.20 radar installed and were known as P.1109As, while XF378 was designated P.1109B. The avionics work was undertaken by the Royal Radar Establishment (RRE) at Defford and both RAE Farnborough and Bedford's High Speed Flight were involved in the flying. WW594 first flew on September 23, 1955, and WW598 on December 31 that year. XF378 was first flown with two Blue Jays and its AI.20 nose radar on September 12, 1956, and in September 1957 it took part in the SBAC Farnborough Show (when the P.1109 configuration was shown for the first time in public).

WW594's take-off weight with its standard Avon 203 engine was 16,810lb (7,625kg) which included 150lb (68kg) of ballast to represent the radar. The highest recorded airspeed was 620kts (714mph/1,149km/h), the maximum recorded Mach number 1.16 (in a steep dive from 51,000ft / 15,545m) and the greatest altitude achieved being 55,000ft (16,764m). The latter was reached in a zoom climb and is officially considered to be the highest altitude ever attained by any Hunter (although CFE test pilot 'Bob' Broad did get a brand-new and very light F.1, without its guns, to almost 57,000ft /17,374m). When test-flown in September 1956, XF378's all-up-weight with two 'uncharged' Blue Jays on the inboard pylons was 17,656lb (8,009kg).

Hawker publicity photo of the Fireflash-armed P.1109B, XF378. (Hawker Aircraft)

After completing its P.1109 role, WW598 was retained for further research with RAE. In due course it was painted in this attractive white colour scheme, and this view may have been taken at RAE's Llanbedr airfield in Wales. (Key)

By 1969, WW598 sported this attractive blue and white scheme, which was very similar to that worn by the Blue Diamonds display team. In 1974 this Hunter was re-purchased by Hawker Siddeley and converted to an FGA.70A for Lebanon. (Adrian Balch)

In conclusion, the P.1109's flying characteristics and behaviour were considered normal for a Hunter, and overall the handling – even at transonic speeds – did not seem to have been appreciably affected by the nose extension, or by the presence of the missiles. In fact, XF378's general manoeuvring with two Blue Jays proved to be 'very satisfactory' and it could also be landed single-handed with one missile remaining, after one had been fired. Two Blue Jays were successfully launched from XF378 in early November 1956, but by the time of the September 1957 Farnborough show, the Hunter/Blue Jay trials were almost finished. Just a few examples of AI.Mk.20 were ever built, all for trials purposes, and the equipment was never used operationally. WW594 was later converted to an FR.10, but WW598 was retained for use by RRE and RAE right through the 1960s, and still with its elongated nose.

There was to be another brief study into a Firestreak-armed Hunter, though. In July 1960 Hawker and de Havilland proposed a simple conversion, which would have the standard Hunter forward fuselage gunpack replaced by a similar self-contained pack with two Firestreaks attached to the sides of the lower forward fuselage. Two months later, however, it was clarified officially that two of the guns must be retained with the missiles and this killed the idea.

One or two Hunters were used for trials work quite late in the type's career. This March 1976 photo shows an airframe engaged in air firings of an Air-to-Air Test Vehicle based on the design for a new Short Range Air-to-Air Missile (SRAAM), then currently under consideration by Hawker Siddeley Dynamics. The SRAAM twin launcher had been adapted to carry one round in the starboard launch tube, while the other carried instrumentation. These air launches were part of a technology development programme to prove, with a limited number of firings, that the predicted performance for the missile could be achieved. (Hawker Siddeley)

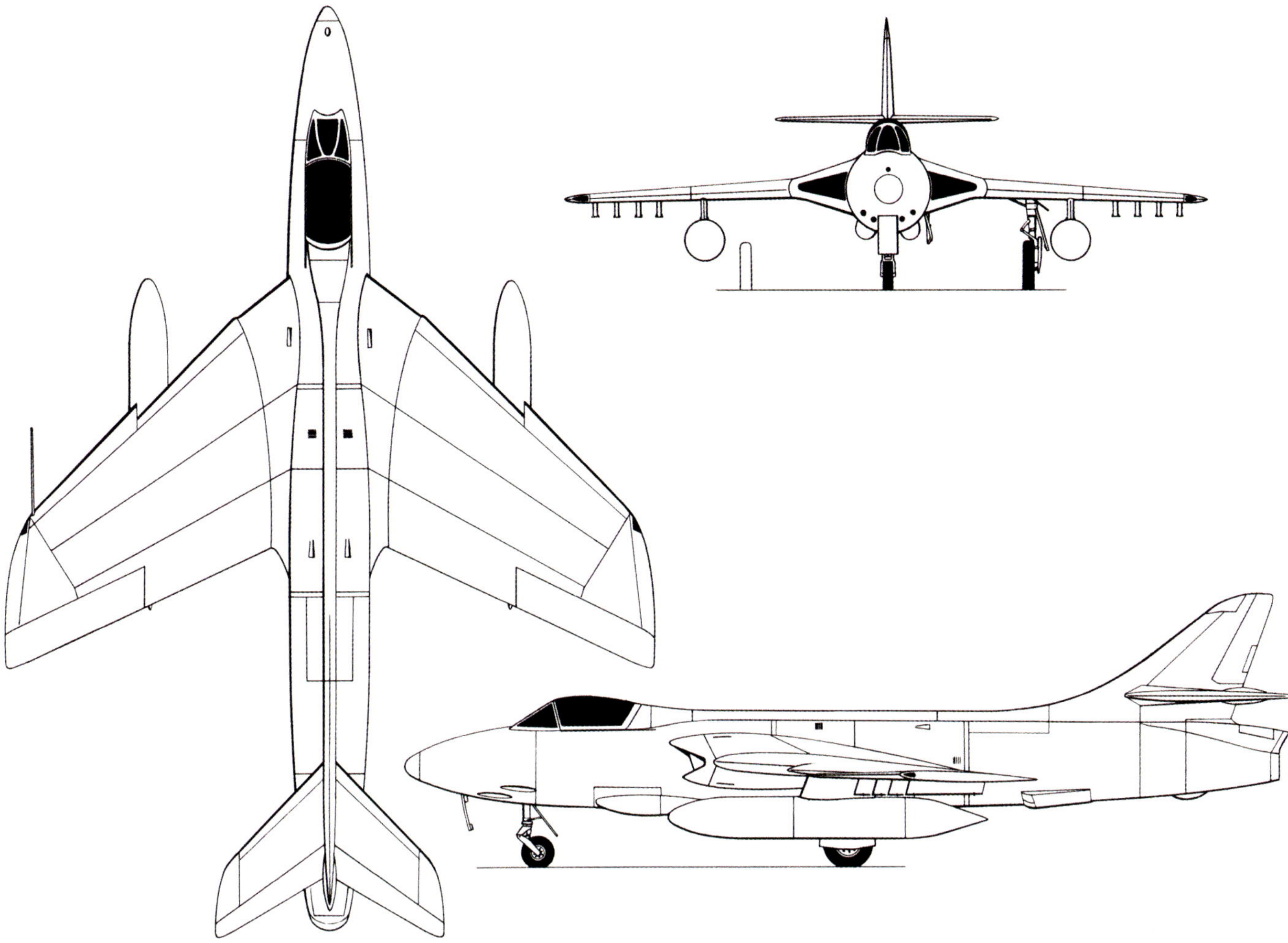

HAWKER HUNTER DATA

Type: Single-seat, single-engined, mid-wing cantilever monoplane interceptor fighter and ground-attack aircraft

Dimensions, all marks

Span: 33ft 8in (10.26m)

Length: 45ft 10 1/2in (13.98m)

Height: 13ft 2in (4.01m)

Gross wing area: 340sq ft (31.62m^2); Mk.6 with extended leading edge 349sq ft (32.46m^2)

Wing aspect ratio: 3.33

Wing thickness/chord ratio: 0.085

Tailplane span: 11ft 10in (3.62m)

Tailplane gross area with elevators: 53.9sq ft (5.01m^2)

Tailplane thickness/chord ratio: 0.080

Wheel track: 14ft 9in (4.5m)

Powerplant

F.1: Rolls-Royce A.J.65 Avon (RA.7 rating) Mk.113 or 115 of 7,500lb (33.3kN) sea level static thrust

F.2 and F.5: Armstrong Siddeley Sapphire Mk.101 (Sa.6) of 8,000lb (35.6kN) sea level static thrust

F.3: A.J.65 Avon (RA.7R), 7,130lb (31.7kN) thrust dry, 9,600lb (42.7kN) with reheat

F.4: Avon AJ.65 (RA.7) Mk.113, 115, 119, 120 or 121, 7,500lb (33.3kN) thrust

F.6: Avon (RA.28) Mk.203, 10,000lb (44.4kN) thrust

FGA.9: Avon 207, 10,050lb (44.7kN)

Maximum internal fuel capacity Mks.4/5/6: 392 gal (1,782 lit) - front fuselage tank 200 gal (909 lit), rear 52 gal (236 lit), eight wing tanks totaling 140 gal (637 lit)

With two 100 gal (455 lit) drop tanks (F.4/5/6): 592 gal (2,692 lit)

With two 230 gal (1,046 lit) drop tanks (FGA.9/FR.10): 852 gal (3,874 lit)

With two 230 and two 100 gal drop tanks: 1,052 gal (4,783 lit)

Empty Weight: F.1 12,128lb (5,501kg), F.2 11,973lb (5,431kg), F.4 12,543lb (5,690kg), F.6 12,760lb (5,788kg)

Maximum loaded weight (clean): F.1 16,200lb (7,348kg), F.2 16,300lb (7,394kg), F.4 17,100lb (7,757kg), F.5 17,000lb (7,711kg), F.6 17,750lb (8,051kg)

Overload weight (1,052 gal/4,783 lit fuel): F.6 23,800lb (10,796kg)

Performance (F.6 clean)

Maximum Mach level flight: 0.95 at 36,000ft (10,973m)

Maximum Mach in a dive: 1.25 (in level flight, Hunter was incapable of supersonic speed but in a shallow dive went supersonic with ease)

Maximum speed at sea level: 621 kts (1,151km/h)

Service ceiling (rate of climb 500ft per min/152m per min): 50,000ft (15,240m)

Absolute ceiling: 52,500ft (16,002m)

Stalling speed in landing configuration: 105 kts (195km/h)

Radius of action (clean): 280 nautical miles (519km)

Radius of action (two 100 gal/455 lit drop tanks): 490nm (908km)

Ferry range (with 1,052 gal/4,783 lit fuel, landing reserves): 1,550nm (2,872km)

HAWKER HUNTER FGA.9

1 Radome
2 Radar scanner dish
3 Ram air intake
4 Camera port
5 Radar ranging equipment
6 Camera access panel
7 Gun camera
8 Ground pressurisation connection
9 Nosewheel door
10 Oxygen bottles
11 IFF aerial
12 Electronics equipment
13 Nosewheel bay
14 De-icing fluid tank
15 Pressurisation control valves
16 Cockpit front bulkhead
17 Nose undercarriage leg
18 Nosewheel forks
19 Forward retracting nosewheel
20 Nosewheel leg door
21 Cannon muzzle port
22 Gun blast cascade deflectors
23 Rudder pedals
24 Bulletproof windscreen
25 Cockpit canopy framing
26 Reflector gun sight
27 Instrument panel shroud
28 Control column
29 Cockpit section fuselage frames
30 Rearward sliding cockpit canopy
31 Pilot's starboard side console
32 Martin-Baker Mk.3H ejection seat
33 Throttle control
34 Pilot's port side console
35 Cannon barrel tubes
36 Pneumatic system air bottles
37 Cockpit canopy emergency release
38 Cockpit rear pressure bulkhead
39 Air conditioning valve
40 Ejection seat headrest
41 Firing handle
42 Air louvres
43 Ammunition tanks
44 Ammunition link collector box
45 Cartridge case ejectors
46 Batteries
47 Port air inlet
48 Boundary layer splitter plate
49 Inlet lip construction
50 Radio and electronics equipment bay
51 Sliding canopy rail
52 Air conditioning supply pipes
53 Control rod linkages
54 Communications aerial
55 Fuselage double frame bulkhead
56 Boundary layer air outlet
57 Secondary air inlet door, spring loaded
58 Inlet duct construction
59 Forward fuselage fuel tank
60 Starboard inlet duct
61 Starboard wing fuel tank
62 230 Imp gal (1,046 lit) drop tank
63 Inboard pylon mounting
64 Leading edge dog-tooth
65 100 Imp gal drop tank
66 Outboard pylon mounting
67 Wing fence
68 Leading edge extension
69 Starboard navigation light
70 Starboard wingtip
71 Whip aerial

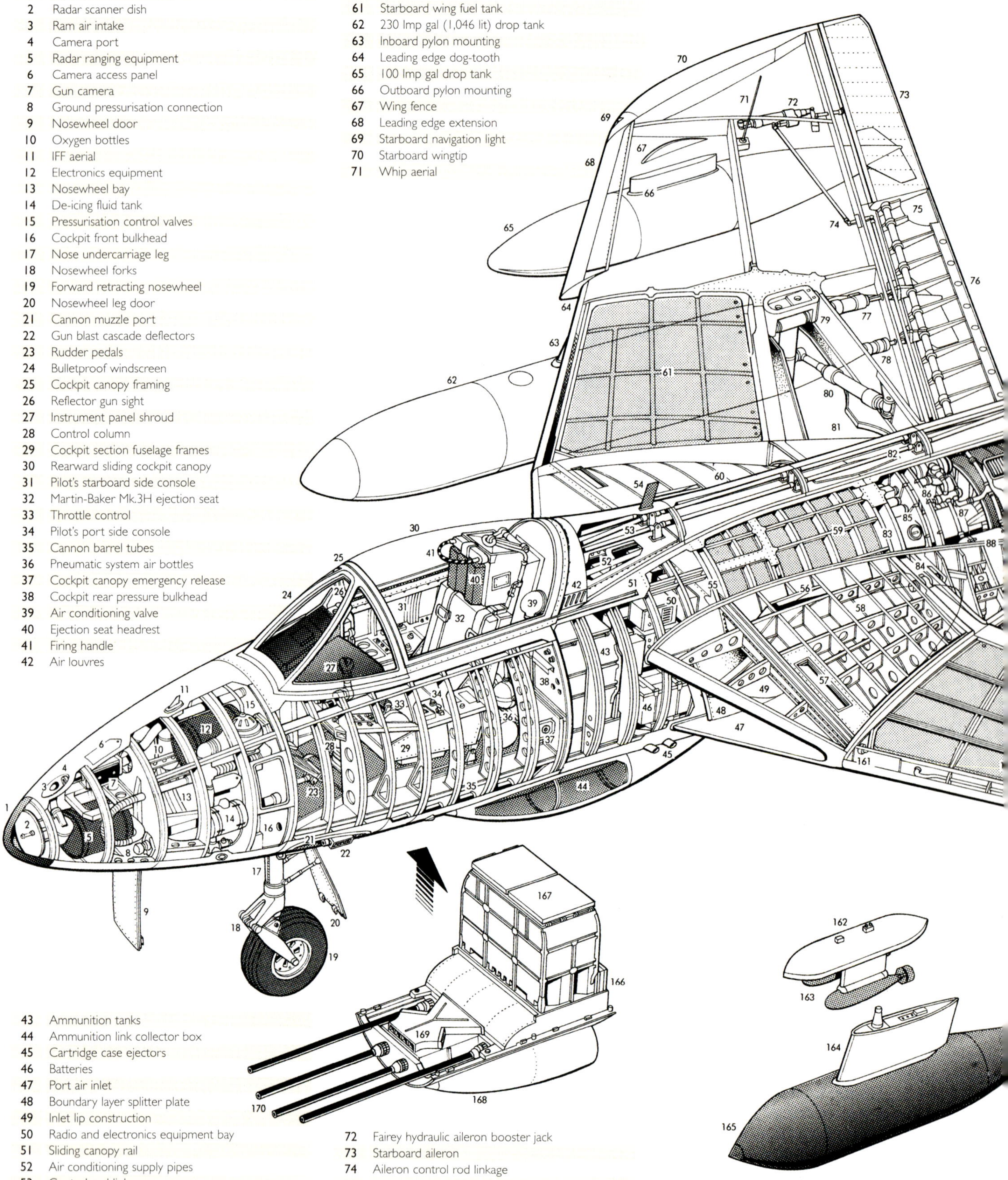

72 Fairey hydraulic aileron booster jack
73 Starboard aileron
74 Aileron control rod linkage
75 Flap cut-out section for drop tank clearance
76 Starboard flap construction
77 Flap hydraulic jack
78 Flap synchronising jack
79 Starboard main undercarriage mounting
80 Retraction jack
81 Starboard undercarriage bay
82 Dorsal spine fairing
83 Main wing attachment frames
84 Main spar attachment joint
85 Engine starter fuel tank
86 Air conditioning system
87 Engine inlet compressor face

88 Air conditioning pre-cooler
89 Cooling air outlet louvres
90 Rear spar attachment frames
91 Aileron control rods
92 Front engine mountings
93 Rolls-Royce Avon 207 engine
94 Bleed-air duct
95 Engine bay cooling flush air intake
96 Rear engine mounting
97 Rear fuselage joint ring
98 Joint ring attachment bolts
99 Tailplane control rods
100 Fuel piping from rear tank
101 Rear fuselage fuel tank
102 Fuel collector tank
103 Jet pipe mounting rail
104 Fin root fairing
105 Hydraulic accumulator
106 Tailplane trim jack

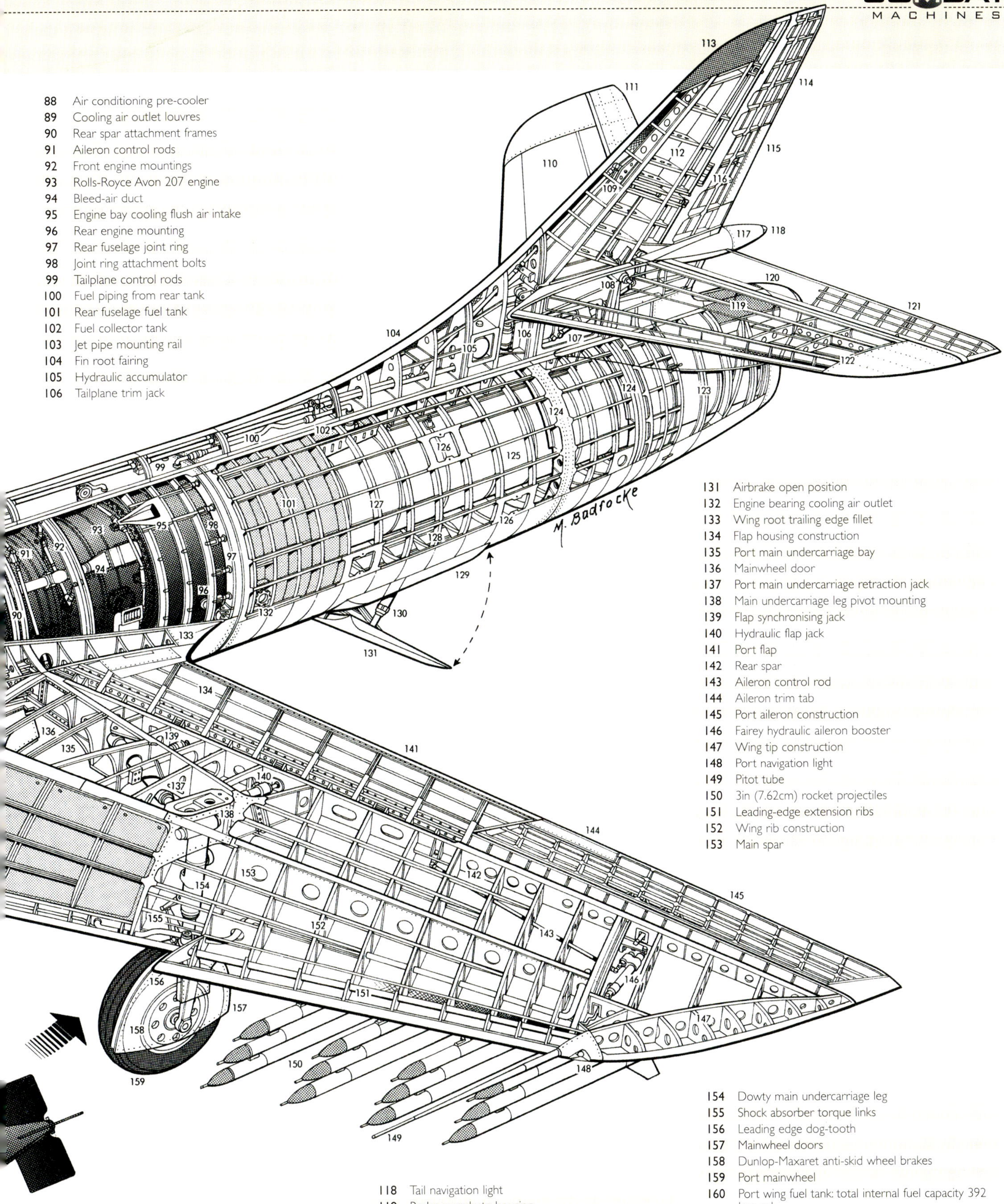

107 Fairey hydraulic elevator booster
108 Tailplane mounting pivot
109 Rudder hinge control rods
110 Starboard tailplane
111 Starboard elevator
112 Fin construction
113 Fin tip aerial fairing
114 Rudder construction
115 Rudder trim tab
116 Trim tab control jack
117 Tailplane anti-buffet fairing
118 Tail navigation light
119 Brake parachute housing
120 Tailplane fairing
121 Port elevator construction
122 Tailplane construction
123 Detachable tailcone
124 Tailplane spar mounting
125 Jet pipe
126 Jet pipe access doors
127 Rear fuselage frame and stringer construction
128 Airbrake jack housing
129 Airbrake retracted position
130 Airbrake operating jack
131 Airbrake open position
132 Engine bearing cooling air outlet
133 Wing root trailing edge fillet
134 Flap housing construction
135 Port main undercarriage bay
136 Mainwheel door
137 Port main undercarriage retraction jack
138 Main undercarriage leg pivot mounting
139 Flap synchronising jack
140 Hydraulic flap jack
141 Port flap
142 Rear spar
143 Aileron control rod
144 Aileron trim tab
145 Port aileron construction
146 Fairey hydraulic aileron booster
147 Wing tip construction
148 Port navigation light
149 Pitot tube
150 3in (7.62cm) rocket projectiles
151 Leading-edge extension ribs
152 Wing rib construction
153 Main spar
154 Dowty main undercarriage leg
155 Shock absorber torque links
156 Leading edge dog-tooth
157 Mainwheel doors
158 Dunlop-Maxaret anti-skid wheel brakes
159 Port mainwheel
160 Port wing fuel tank: total internal fuel capacity 392 Imp gal
161 Leading edge pin joint
162 ML twin stores carrier
163 20lb (9kg) practice bombs
164 Inboard wing pylon
165 1,000lb bomb
166 Four 30mm Aden gun pack
167 Ammunition boxes, 100 rounds per gun
168 Link collector box
169 Gun gas purging air duct
170 Cannon barrels remaining in aircraft when gun pack is withdrawn

Swiss Hunter F.58 J-4007 in Fliegerstaffeln 7 colours, photographed during an April 1989 training course. The scheme was apparently applied for just three days. (Key)

SUCCESS ABROAD

Hawker's factories built large numbers of Hunters for export, and further contracts were awarded to Belgian and Dutch manufacturers for licenced construction. Many ex-RAF and foreign-built airframes were also refurbished for sale around the world

Abu Dhabi

The Abu Dhabi Army Air Wing received seven Hunter FGA.76s (ex-RAF F.4 variants refurbished to FGA.9 standard) in 1970 to equip one squadron. These were followed in 1971 by three FR.76As and a pair of two-seat T.77 trainers. Some single-seaters were then later transferred to Somalia in Africa.

Abu Dhabi T.77, 711, in the 1960s. The camouflage was Dark Earth and Middle Stone over a vivid sky blue, with a red cheatline.

Belgium

Belgium and Holland co-operated in a joint programme to build the Hunter under licence, the British fighter winning an evaluation against the Canadair Sabre and Dassault Mystère IVA. Avions Fairey and SABCA in Belgium, along with Fokker in the Netherlands, built F.4s and F.6s with their Rolls-Royce Avon engines manufactured by Fabrique Nationale at Herstal, Belgium. That country never acquired two-seaters because its pilots were trained in Holland.

The first Belgian-assembled example (ID-2) joined 7 Escadrille (Squadron) at Chièvres in August 1956; 7 Wing embraced 7, 8 and 9 Escadrilles, while 1 and 9 Wings (at Beauvechain and Bierset) commanded 349 and 350 Escadrilles, and 22 and 26 Escadrilles respectively. Wings 1 and 9 lost their F.4s in 1958 and 1959 and 7 Wing's in 1960. In 1958 some SABCA-built F.4s were upgraded to partial F.6 standard but they could not take the Avon 200. The first F.6 was delivered in May 1957, and 7 and 9 Wings acquired examples from December and September 1957. No 9 Wing lost its Hunters in 1960 but 7 Wing kept them operational for ground-attack work. No 8 Squadron also served as a Hunter Operational Conversion Unit but was disbanded in August 1963, 7 Squadron following in November 1963. Belgian squadron codes were (7 Wing) '7J' for 7 Escadrille, 'OV' for 8 Escadrille and 'S2' for 9 Escadrille, and (9 Wing) 'IS' for 22 Escadrille and 'JE' for 26 Escadrille.

Chile

Between September 1966 and mid-1968, Chile received 15 FGA.71s (Mk.9

Belgian Air Force Hunter IF-61 'OV-W' of 8 Escadrille within 7 Wing, at Chièvres in 1960. (Key)

standard) converted by Hawker from ex-Belgian, Dutch and RAF F.6s. These were followed by three more FR.71As (FR.10 standard) and seven T.72s (second P.1101 standard). From 1970 a further 16 F.71s were acquired, all being ex-RAF F.4s/F.6s, and from 1982 another 15, although some of the latter were for spares only. Ground-attack and trainer versions flew with Grupo 8 and the reconnaissance Hunters joined Grupo 9, both based at Antofagasta.

Denmark

The Royal Danish Air Force had 30 standard F.4s delivered from Kingston as F.51s from November 1955. These all joined 724 Squadron (Esk-724) at Aalborg (later Karup and then Skrydstrup) and were followed in 1958 by two T.53s, with two more in 1967. No. 724 Squadron did not disband until March 1974. Denmark's Hunters were initially finished in standard RAF colours, but they later appeared in overall green paint.

India

This large Asian country ordered 160 F.56s (F.6s), the first 32 of which were airframes earmarked for the RAF but cancelled while on the production line, and then cleared by the Ministry of Supply for the new customer. The next 16 came directly from RAF stocks. India's first example was delivered in October 1957. All new-build F.56s had gun blast deflectors and tail parachutes, and some could carry 230 gal (1,046 lit) drop tanks. A further 22 T.66s followed with Avon 203s, the first being delivered in February 1959. Between 1966 and 1970 another 53 F.56As were supplied (Hawker refurbishments to Mk.9 standard from ex-Belgian and RAF), in 1966 also came 12 T.66Ds and in 1973, five T.66Es (all ex-F.6s)

The first unit to fly the Hunter was 7 Squadron at Ambala, which operated the F.56 from December 1957 to

A Belgian Air Force F.6, coded IF-13. This aircraft was later converted to Indian F.56A serial A463. (All Tony Buttler unless stated)

The first Chilean two-seat T.72, J-718, in attractive four-tone camouflage. (Key)

June 1973. This was followed by 14 and 20 Squadrons at Kalaikunda (both from 1958), 27 at Ambala (September 1958-1970s), 17 at Poona (from 1958) and 37 at Kalaikunda (from 1959). India's Hunter force was concentrated into two wings based at Ambala and Poona, each of which comprised three squadrons. Every unit also received two trainers and in addition an Operational Conversion Unit at Ambala, comprising single- and two-seat Hunters.

Replacement of the type by the Jaguar in 14 Squadron began in 1979 and for 27 Squadron during 1985, but the process of phasing out the Hunter was very slow. Examples were retained for weapons training and as target tugs by 3 and 31 Squadrons within the Armament Training Wing based at Jamnagar. A Target Tug Flight was formed at Kalaikunda in 1972 and it was this unit that operated India's very last Hunters. A number of India's aircraft were lost in wars with Pakistan.

Iraq

Iraq initially purchased 15 Hunter F.6s from RAF stocks, paid for with American funding. The Arab nation's first Hunter squadron was duly formed at Habbaniya in spring 1958, and its pilots were trained by the RAF's 229 OCU in the UK. Another 46 former Belgian and Dutch F.6s were supplied by Hawker between 1964 and 1967, comprising 24 FGA.59s, 18 FGA.59As and four FGA.59Bs, and all were upgraded to Mk.9 standard. The two-seat element comprised Hawker's demonstration aircraft G-APUX on loan from 1963 (and later to Jordan and Lebanon), plus five T.69s, all ex-Belgian F.6s with new noses. Iraq's Hunters became involved in several wars over three decades. Serial numbers were painted on the rear fuselage in Arabic numerals.

Jordan

In 1958 the Royal Jordanian Air Force placed orders for 12 F.6s to equip I Squadron, which formed at Mafraq in November. These were all ex-RAF machines, as were another 12 FGA.9s (F.73s) acquired in 1962 to equip 2 Squadron, and two FR.10s in 1960. One F.6 and two more FGA.9s (all ex-RAF) arrived in 1967 and two more FGA.73s in 1968. No 6 Operational Conversion Unit flew single and two-seaters after a new-build T.66B (Avon 200) was supplied by Hawker in 1960, along with two more converted ex-Dutch F.6s. G-APUX also came on loan. Four F.73As arrived in 1969 (ex-RAF as full Mk.9s) with nine more following in 1971, along with three Mk.73Bs. Two ex-Saudi T.70s also joined the fleet in 1968. These later orders replaced war losses and the Hunter was finally retired from service in 1974. Some survivors went to Oman.

An Iraqi F.59 shown at the start of its delivery flight from the UK in 1964. (Hawker Siddeley)

India's A484 was an F.56A but when pictured here, near the end of that country's Hunter service, it was in use as a target-towing aircraft.

Kuwaiti F.57 serial 212 at Dunsfold in 1965, just before delivery. (Hawker Siddeley)

Kenya
In 1974 and early 1975, four FGA.80s (FGA.9) and a T.81, all refurbished RAF single-seaters, came to Kenya from Hawker Siddeley as a counter to then recently strengthened neighbouring air arms. A T.8C was acquired in 1973 and they were based at Nanyuki, but in 1981 the survivors were passed to Zimbabwe. Kenyan Hunters wore standard RAF Dark Green and Dark Sea Grey camouflage on their upper surfaces, with Light Aircraft Grey on the undersides.

Kuwait
Kuwait acquired a few Hunters in 1965-67 and another in 1969, with oilfield defence in mind. These comprised four FGA.57s (FGA.9 standard) converted by Kingston from Belgian and RAF F.6s ,and one FGA.9, plus four T.67s converted from F.6s.

Lebanon
Israel's neighbour acquired five ex-RAF F.6s as FGA.70s in 1958, while in 1965-66, Kingston converted another four Belgian airframes to FGA.9 standard, still as Mk.70s. Another six ex-UK machines were refurbished as FGA.70As in 1975 and 1977. Three T.66Cs (Belgian F.6s) were delivered in 1965-66 and Lebanon also leased G-APUX in 1965.

Netherlands
Royal Netherlands Air Force Hunters were built under licence by Fokker and funded by the US government's Offshore Procurement Program (as were Belgium's Hunters). To begin, 96 F.4s were constructed with the first leaving the factory in February 1956, and the last in November 1957. Another 93 F.6s followed between October 1957-1959, plus 20 T.7s from July 1958 – the first ten of the latter were home-built, with the rest coming from a cancelled RAF order. Dutch Hunters took part in major NATO exercises, they operated with NATO's Second Allied Tactical Air Force, and occasionally intercepted Soviet bombers. Belgian and Dutch pilots were jointly converted to type, using the latter's two-seaters (the reason why Belgium never bought trainers). Low flying training was also conducted at Goose Bay in Canada with RNethAF Hunters deploying there annually. Six squadrons flew Hunters...

This Jordanian F.6 was photographed at Farnborough.

British military serial XM126 was used for a two-seat Hunter delivered to the Royal Netherlands Air Force where it was serialled N-320. From 1966 this aircraft was employed by the Dutch National Air and Space Laboratory as PH-NLH until retirement in 1980. It is seen here at Greenham Common, June 1979. (Chris Goss)

322 at Soesterberg had F.4s in 1958 only, with F.6s arriving from April 1958 and operating until April 1960. However, this unit re-equipped on the F.4 again in May 1960, when its fighters were taken by the aircraft carrier *Karel Doorman* to the island of Biak to provide air defence during the bitter Indonesian Confrontation in Dutch New Guinea. F.6s arrived in December 1961 and these could carry 230 gal (1,046 lit) tanks rather than the F.4's 100 gal (455 lit) capacity, although 322 Squadron flew both versions until September 1962.

F.4s joined 323 Squadron at Leeuwarden in October 1957, when the unit's role was air-to-air gunnery training. Through 1959-60 they would tow banner targets until this task became the responsibility of the Flight Service Squadron. Further Hunters were allocated to a Conversion Flight, which joined 323 in late 1959. The latter's Hunters were withdrawn in 1963, while 324 Squadron flew the F.4 for a very short period because it was the first unit to switch to the F.6, in October 1957, flying that sub-type at Leeuwarden until 1964.

No 325 Squadron, also at Leeuwarden, was the first F.4 unit, from December 1955, and after moving to Soesterberg it received F.6s from September 1958. Next, 326 Squadron at Woensdrecht began conversion to the F.4 in November 1957. It switched to F.6s in 1960, having that year moved to Soesterberg, but was disbanded in December 1961. The F.4 also reached 327 Squadron at Volkel in 1957, but in January 1958 this unit was merged with 322 Squadron. The last operational F.4 flight was made in Holland in August 1963, and the last Dutch Air Force Hunter, a 325 Squadron aircraft, was retired in August 1968. However, T.7 N-320 became civil register PH-NLH to conduct research with the Lucht-en-Ruimtevaartlaboratorium (National Air and Space Laboratory). It was retired in January 1980.

Dutch Hunters used similar colours to RAF machines with Dark Sea Grey and Dark Green upper surfaces and High Speed Silver undersides. The T.7s were painted overall silver with Day-Glo areas on the nose, rear fuselage and wing tips. Initially, 322 Squadron used '3W' codes for each of its aircraft, 323 Squadron 'Y9' codes, 324 '3P' codes, 325 '4R' codes, 326 '9I' and 327 '7E' codes. The use of these devices lasted until late 1959, when they gradually began to disappear to be replaced by N-serial numbers.

Oman

The Sultanate of Oman Air Force received 40 Hunters of mixed variants, many coming from Jordan in 1975 but supplemented by examples from Kuwait and conversions from the UK. These were formed into 6 Squadron based at Thumrait, and the survivors were retired in August 1993.

Peru

Peru's Air Force ordered 16 F.52s (ex-RAF F.4s) and from 1956 these equipped one squadron within Grupo 12 (Escuadron de Caza 14) at Limatambo, and from 1957 Talara (other units within the Grupo flew American fighters). A single T.62 (ex-RAF F.4) was delivered in October 1959. Hunter flying abated from 1968 following a switch to ground-attack duties, but did not end completely until 1992.

Qatar

Three FGA.78s and one T.79, all ex-Dutch F.6s and a T.7, were delivered to Qatar in December 1971, and were used until the 1980s.

Rhodesia/Zimbabwe

Rhodesia acquired 12 ex-RAF F.6s, updated to FGA.9 standard, between December 1962 and April 1963 to equip 1 Squadron at Thornhill.

A Kenyan Air Force Hunter at Luqa, Malta, in 1974. Note the large blade aerial behind the canopy. (Key)

A delightful air-to-air study of Royal Netherlands Air Force F.4 N-176, of 323 Squadron at Leeuwarden. (Key)

After independence, Zimbabwe bought four more FGA.9s and a T.7 from Kenya, and another nine Mk.9s came from Britain in 1984 and 1987. For security during anti-guerilla operations, the air force changed the serials of many of its aircraft, and its Hunters carried random numbers in the 1xxx and 8xxx series. Rhodesian Hunters, and those of the Air Force of Zimbabwe, were given camouflage of Dark Green and Dark Earth.

Saudi Arabia

Four refurbished ex-RAF F.6s and two T.7s were delivered to Saudi Arabia in 1966, to serve as lead-in aircraft to the complex and more powerful Lightning, ordered at the same time. The survivors were presented to Jordan in 1968.

Singapore

The Republic of Singapore Air Force received 12 FGA.74s and four FR.74As (ex-RAF F.6s modified to Mk.9/10 standards) in 1970-71 after the nation had acquired independence. These equipped 140 and 141 Squadrons based at Tengah, within the island's Air Defence Command. Another eight former RAF F.4s and 14 F.6s were supplied in 1972-73 along with four T.75s and five T.75As in 1970 and 1972-73. Most single-seaters were equipped to carry AIM-9 Sidewinder air-to-air missiles.

Somalia

A quantity of Hunters, at least ten, were supplied to Somalia by Abu Dhabi in 1983 and used for approximately six years.

Sweden

The Svenska Flygvapnet ordered 120 F.50s (F.4s) with Avon 115s direct from Hawker, the type entering service as the J 34 with F 18 Wing at Södertörn in August 1955 (more powerful Avon 119s and 120s were fitted later). The objective was to fill an air-defence gap between the J 29 Tunnan and the forthcoming supersonic J 35 Draken, with Hunters operating as day interceptors against bombers flying at high altitude; later these aircraft were modified to carry Sidewinders. The Flygvapnet used Wings or Flygflottilj comprising three Squadrons, 1, 2 and 3, and these were identified by a colour, respectively Red, Blue and Yellow, while the staff aircraft for a wing was marked with white. Sweden's F.50s sported dark green upper surfaces and sky blue undersides, and no example had a saw tooth leading-edge mainplane.

In October 1956, F 8 at Barkarby became the second wing to receive J 34s, keeping them until disbandment in spring 1961. F 8's Hunters then joined F 9 Wing at Säve in 1962, later moving to Ängelholm. With the arrival of the Draken, F 18 Wing's Hunters (then at Tullinge) also went to F 9 and to F 10 Wings at Säve, where they lasted until 1969. However, just 2 Squadron

Sultanate of Oman Air Force FGA.73B '841' as seen on November 8, 1980, in its effective low-visibility grey colour scheme.

Swedish J 34 34016 arrived at F 18 Wing in 1956.

of F 10 Wing used the J 34, from 1963-1967. Most Swedish Hunters were scrapped, just four returning to Kingston for rebuild into Swiss T.68s. Sweden never bought the two-seater.

Flight trials began in 1958 using Hunter 34085 fitted with a Svenska Flygmotor afterburner as a J 34 B; this refit included small additional mid-fuselage dorsal intakes. The aircraft's time-to-height was reduced drastically, with just four minutes needed to reach 39,370ft (12,000m); rate of turn was improved, but the afterburner flamed out at 42,000ft (12,800m) and so could not contribute to reaching higher altitudes. The programme was abandoned, though, in part because of the engine's high fuel consumption.

Switzerland

The Schweizer Luftwaffe ordered 100 F.58s (F.6s) with an additional tail parachute and enlarged ammunition link containers. The first 12 were ex-RAF but the rest new-build, with deliveries between 1958-1960. A further order followed for 52 F.58As (F.4s, F.6s and GA.11s, and two T.7s, upgraded to Mk.9 standard) all delivered in 1971-75, in many cases in kit form for assembly at the Federal Aircraft Factory at Emmen. Most had provision to carry two AIM-9 Sidewinders on underwing pylons. Finally, eight T.68 trainers were delivered in 1974-75, half being modified RAF Mk.4s and the remainder ex-Swedish Mk.50s.

Their service was extensive and in 1990 the Hunter still equipped Fliegerstaffeln 2 at Ulrichen, 3 (Ambri), 5 and 9 (Raron), 7 (Interlaken), 15 (St Stephan), 20 (Mollis), 21 (Turtmann) and 22 (Ulrichen and St Stephan). Previously Fliegerstaffeln 1, 4, 8, 11, 18 and 19 had also been equipped with Hunters and the airfield list included Dubendorf and Meiringen, with trainers based at Turtmann. And if their runways were unserviceable due to enemy action, these Hunters could also use adjacent motorways as improvised bases/runways. Hunter pilot training at emergency operational locations such as these, deep in the Alpine region of central Switzerland, took place twice a year to enable them to retreat to more secure positions in the event of invasion. They would be defended by anti-aircraft guns and surface-to-air missiles. The last in-service flight by a Swiss Hunter, in fact by F.58 J-4001, took place in December 1994.

This Chilean Air Force FGA.71 is loaded with practice bombs on its port outboard pylon, and a rocket pod on the equivalent pylon to starboard. It has also been fitted with chaff/flare dispensers on its rear fuselage. (Key)

OVERSEAS AIR ARMS PRODUCTION LIST

Hunter F.58 'Papyrus', Fliegerstaffel 15, Swiss Air Force, St Stephan, 1993.

(Refurbished airframes mostly Kingston)

Abu Dhabi

FGA.76 (7) Serials 701-707

FR.76A (3) 708-710

T.77 (2) 711, 712

Belgium

F.4 (112) ID-1 to ID-64 (all assembled in Belgium except ID-1 from Kingston as pattern), ID-101 to ID-148

F.6 (144) IF-1 to IF-144 (Belgium and Holland manufacture)

Chile

FGA.71 (28 + 15) J-700 to J-714, J-724 to J-735, J-737, J-738, J-740 to J-754

FR.71A (3) J-715 to J-717

T.72 (7) J-718 to J-723, J-736

Denmark

F.51 (30 all Kingston-built airframes) E-401 to E-430 (first 21 originally 401-421)

T.53 (4) ET-271 to ET-274

India

F.56 (160 Kingston) BA201-BA360 (BA201-BA248 ex-RAF)

T.66 (22 Kingston) BS361-BS376, BS485-BS490

F.56A (53) A459-A494, A936-A943, A967-969, A1010-A1015

T.66D (12) S-570 to S-581

T.66E (5) S-1389 to S-1393

Iraq

F.6 (15) 394-398, 400-409

FGA.59 (24) 570-587, 628-633

FGA.59A (18) 657-661, 690-702

FGA.59B (4) 662-665

T.69 (6) 567 (G-APUX), 567-569, 626, 627

Jordan

F.6 (13) 700-711, 717

FR.10 (2) 853, 712

F.73/FGA.9 (16) 801-812, 825, 826, 814, 832

F.73A (13) 828-831, 840, 842-849

F.73B (3) 841, 850, 851

T.66A (1) 800 (G-APUX)

T.66B (3) 714, 716, 718

T.70 (2) 835, 836

Kenya

FGA.80 (4) 803-806

T.81 (1) 801

T.8C (1) 802

Kuwait

FGA.57 (4) 212-215

FGA.6/FGA.9 (2 & 1) 216, 217, 220

T.67 (4) 210, 211, 218, 219

Lebanon

FGA.70/FGA.9 (5 & 4) L-170 to L179

F.6 (6) L-280 to L-285 (first five originally L-180 to L-184)

T.66A (1) L-581 (G-APUX)

T.66C (3) Initially L-286 to L-288, later L-280 to L-282

Netherlands

F.4 (96 all Fokker) N-101 to N-196

F.6 (93 all Fokker) N-201 to N-293

T.7 (20 – first 10 Fokker, remainder Kingston) N-301 to N-320

Oman

FGA.73/73A/73B (35) 718-725, 815-817, 825-832, 840-854

T.66B (3) 800-802

T.67 (2) 803, 804

Peru

F.52 (16) 630-645

T.62 (1) 681

Qatar

FGA.78 (3) QA-10 to QA-12

T.79 (1) QA-13

Rhodesia/Zimbabwe

FGA.9/80 (25) – first 12 RRAF 116-127; later random four-digit numbers on all

T.7/81 (1) 1084

Saudi Arabia

F.60 (4) 60-601 to 60-604

T.70 (2) 70-616, 70-617

Singapore

FGA.74 (12) 501, 502, 505, 507-511, 513, 515, 518, 519

FR.74 (4) 503, 506, 512, 517

FR.74B (22) 520-527, 529, 530, 531, 533-535, 537-539, 541-543, 545, 546

T.75 (4) 500, 504, 514, 516

T.75A (5) 528, 532, 536, 540, 544

Somalia

FGA.76/76A (9?) CC-701 to CC-707, CC-709, CC-710

T.77 (1) CC-711

Sweden

F.50/J 34 (120 - first 24 Kingston, remainder Blackpool) 34001-34120

Switzerland

F.58 (100 all Kingston) J-4001 to J-4100

F.58A (52) J-4101 to J-4152

T.68 (8) J-4201 to J-4208

INTO ACTION

RAF Hunter F.5s from 1 and 34 Squadrons were detached to Nicosia, Cyprus, as part of the support force for Britain's involvement in the Suez Campaign of autumn 1956. For 1 Squadron this excursion lasted from September 1 until just before Christmas, with 34 arriving in October. On November 2 these aircraft flew top-cover sorties over the Canal Zone to support Royal Navy ground-attack aircraft, but the Hunter's limited endurance restricted their time in the patrol area and they did not repeat this duty. Instead, the main task of the Hunters in this theatre became fighter defence for Cyprus in cooperation with French Mystère IVAs, as a counter to the Egyptian Air Force attacking the island with its Ilyushin Il-28 jet bombers.

Once again, the Hunter's range performance, especially regarding its ground-attack potential, was criticised strongly and the RAF became somewhat envious of French Republic F-84F long-range fighter-bombers, which could attack targets in Egypt directly from Cyprus. It was clear the Hunter was a vastly superior aircraft in the high-altitude interceptor role, having an infinitely better ceiling,

XK150/A of 8 Squadron pictured in the early 1960s, soon after its conversion to FGA.9 standard.

Hunter FR.10 XE589/RC, of 1417 Flight RAF, in action during the Radfan Campaign. This sub-unit was formed in March 1963, from the fighter-recce element of 8 Squadron, and was re-absorbed into 8 Squadron proper in September 1967. (All Tony Buttler unless stated)

climb and turn performance, but the need for the F.6 with its greater range become even more important.

RAF Middle East

On June 25, 1961, the Iraqi Prime Minister declared that Kuwait was an integral part of Iraq. In response, Britain began to move forces into Kuwait to counter a possible surprise attack or invasion. Iraq had Hunter F.6s of its own, but the British build up in July included the Hunters of 8 and 208 Squadrons, the limited hard-standing area at Kuwait's airport becoming full of fast jets. The crisis eventually passed, though, and the biggest problem for the Hunter units to overcome, after having maintained high readiness for more than a week, was the severe desert climate.

After the Kuwait emergency, late in 1961 Middle East Command's two FGA.9 squadrons were formed into a single tactical unit called the Khormaksar Wing. The two squadrons then operated on a rotational basis between Bahrain and Khormaksar, staying for a month on each visit; those at Bahrain as a counter to further threats against Kuwait, while the aircraft at Khormaksar covered Britain's commitments in the Western Aden Protectorate and in East Africa as a whole. Aden then became the Headquarters of the RAF's Middle East Command.

The first operations within this role came in January and February 1962 when Hunters (and Avro Shackletons) dropped 1,000lb (454kg) bombs

Hunter FGA.9 XF431/Q of the Khormaksar Strike Wing, wearing joint 8 and 43 Squadron markings.

XF429/X, an FR.10 from 8 Squadron, with four fuel tanks under the wings. (Chris Goss)

and a very large number of 20lb (9.1kg) fragmentation bombs on dissident villages. In September 1962 the new Imam of the Yemen began a strong campaign of propaganda against the Federation of South Arabia, calling for tribes to rebel and overthrow the Federation. Relations between Yemen and both the Federation of South Arabia and the UK gradually deteriorated, and 43 Squadron moved to Khormaksar in March 1963. From October that year, in deterrent flights known as Flag Waves, two Hunters would fly over specified areas at heights above 1,500ft (457m), outside the range of small arms, but without making any attacks. This proved effective for a while.

Then in December 1963 a state of emergency was declared after the number of attacks by Yemen-backed dissidents in the Radfan area began to rise. For the first time, Hunters were used to make cannon and rocket attacks against these terrorists. In March 1964 the Army moved into the Radfan to begin Operation 'Nutcracker', with air support for the ground troops coming from, particularly, the Khormaksar Wing Hunters. Over a two-month period they flew more than 300 strike sorties and 100-plus reconnaissance missions as the enemy was slowly pushed back. Operating with the Khormaksar Wing Squadrons was 1417 Flight equipped with the FR.10, and these aircraft proved especially valuable because they could take detail photos of targets in areas where the available maps were not always of the best quality.

The Radfan, an area of approximately 20 x 15 miles (32 x 24km), provided a stiff test for the Hunter. This was the dissident tribes' primary stronghold and lay some 35 miles (56km) to the north of Aden. It was rocky and had peaks rising above 6,000ft (1,829m), which were then split by deep and often sheer-sided wadis. These features could produce substantial turbulence and sudden alterations in the weather and wind conditions, which at times severely tested the flying skills of the Hunter pilots.

The incursions increased still further and began to involve Yemeni helicopters, with MiG-17 fighters as escorts. In response to one such attack, on March 28 eight Hunters smashed a Harib fort just over the border in Yemen. During April, 43 and 208 Squadrons flew a limited number of ground support sorties, and in May this was followed by a more systematic campaign to destroy targets as the ground offensive gathered momentum. Then, on June 7 the fighting in the Radfan reached its peak, literally, with a major assault against Jebel Huriyah,

These FGA.9s of the Khormaksar Strike Wing, again wearing joint 8/43 Squadron markings, patrol the area's hostile terrain. (Key)

a 6,125ft (1,867m) high mountain that dominated the entire Radfan. All day, endless Hunter attacks and artillery fire brought heavy enemy casualties and in the end the Battle of Jebel Huriyah proved decisive. Afterwards the volume of air operations was reduced, but between April 30 and June 30, 1964, 43 and 208 Squadrons launched 2,500 rocket projectiles in 527 sorties. Offensive operations over the Radfan by Khormaksar Wing Hunters ended on November 18.

The Hunter's contribution had proved invaluable. The FGA.9 was reliable and highly manoeuvrable (having constantly to pull 7g over the Radfan) and it was an excellent weapons platform. The Aden cannon proved accurate and devastating against 'soft-skinned' targets, while the 3in (76mm) rocket projectile could deal with stone buildings such as forts and houses. Along with its regular recce work, including pre- and post-strike photography, the FR.10 was also used to drop leaflets prior to a strike. A big problem, however, was sand, which quickly abraded the Hunter's canopies and necessitated the frequent changing of windscreens.

In January 1966 the British Government announced it was to withdraw its forces from South Arabia, which itself would be granted independence not later than 1968. But fierce fighting broke out between the rival factions wishing to take control of the region, while at the same time Yemen/Egypt-backed dissidents began to attack urban areas of Aden State. For some months from January onwards the Khormaksar Wing Hunters flew air-defence patrols along the border with Yemen, while also having to support further ground action in the Radfan. For example, on August 28, 1966, the Wing attacked and destroyed the enemy fort at Shurjan with rocket projectiles and 30mm ammunition.

In September 1967, 8 Squadron moved to Muharraq, while 1417 Flight was disbanded. However, 43 remained at Khormaksar and continued its ground-attack support sorties, the last of which took place on November 9. The British withdrawal was covered by Royal Navy aircraft operating from the carrier HMS *Eagle* and this allowed 43 Squadron to be disbanded. However, 8 and 208 Squadrons continued as the Offensive Support Wing at Muharraq until 1971, when the final British withdrawal from the Arabian Gulf theatre was completed.

One of the Hunter FR.10s of 1417(FR) Flight, based at Khormaksar, was XF429/KS seen here in mid-1967. (Key)

RAF Far East

Another 'event' that would bring RAF Hunters into action was the Indonesian Confrontation of

Armourers fit rocket rails to a 208 Squadron Hunter. The unit was based at Khormaksar, but here the aircraft is on detachment to Amman in Jordan. (Key)

Hunters of 208 Squadron taxi to the runway at Amman, Jordan, in a view that shows the hot conditions experienced by the groundcrews. (Key)

1962-63. In May 1961 Great Britain proposed a new federation that would embrace Malaya, Singapore, Sarawak, North Borneo and Brunei, but nearby Indonesia opposed this idea very strongly. Then in December 1962 there was a revolt in Brunei. British troops were flown into the area and on December 13 the Hunter FGA.9s of 20 Squadron (plus Canberras from 45 Squadron) were moved from Tengah to Labuan. The Hunters immediately made firing passes over captured buildings at Seria, and within a week this revolt had been repulsed. But it marked the start of four long years of continuous operations by British ground forces, against Indonesia's efforts to stop Sarawak and North Borneo (later known as Sabah) becoming part of the State of Malaysia.

In March 1963 Indonesian guerrillas started to make cross-border raids, and these were increased once the Federation of Malaysia had been formed in September. At selected times 20 Squadron's Hunters were deployed to Labuan and Kuching, while Indonesia announced it would employ air and naval forces to support the insurgents. There were instances of the Indonesian Air Force's older piston-powered F-51 Mustang fighters and B-25 Mitchell bombers infringing Malaysian airspace, but the real worry were the fast jets operated by Indonesia…MiG-17 fighters and Ilyushin Il-28 bombers. Consequently, the Hunters, and some Gloster Javelin FAW.9R night and all-weather fighters, began to fly low-level patrols along the Indonesian border. In fact, an Air Defence Identification Zone was established around the Sabah and Sarawak borders, which stretched three miles (5km) offshore. To police this, four 20 Squadron Hunters were sent to Labuan and four more to Kuching; each base also received two 60 Squadron Javelins, thereby ensuring all-weather air defence was available around the clock.

In a further escalation, in August 1964, Indonesian forces invaded the Malay Peninsula, and attacks were also made against Malaysian patrol vessels and other facilities. Once again, the Hunters switched to ground-attack mode and from September 3, 20 Squadron's aircraft used cannon and rockets to attack enemy paratroopers well concealed in jungle hideouts. After a few days this particular 'invasion' had been completely defeated with many casualties among the invaders, but further regular landings and other attacks by Indonesian forces continued until the end of March 1965. The effort needed to counter these threats placed 20 Squadron's aircraft in continuous operations either engaging ground forces, supporting friendly soldiers, or on other tasks such as coastal reconnaissance.

XE618/L at Muharraq, an FGA.9 with 208 Squadron from mid-1965 until mid-1967. At the end of 1967 this aircraft was transferred to the Kuwaiti Air Force. (Chris Goss)

At the same time, more Indonesian ground forces would regularly cross the Kalimantan border and these jungle missions increased during 1965. In fact, this proved to be the main Indonesian thrust within Borneo, but here the RAF Hunter's involvement was rather limited. Indonesian activity along the Kalimantan border began to fall away during 1966, partly because Indonesia's leader Sukarno was coming under growing international pressure to end the ongoing Confrontation. A peace treaty was finally signed between Malaysia and Indonesia on August 11, 1966.

FGA.9s of 208 Squadron on February 26, 1964. Note the earlier style of unit markings.

Another 208 Squadron aircraft, XE532/K, in 1966.

Dutch activity

Some time earlier, but due to growing concerns over Indonesian intentions, in May 1960 the Netherlands Air Force's 322 Squadron and its Hunter F.4s were embarked on the carrier *Karel Doorman* and ferried to the island of Biak to provide air defence. However, in these tropical conditions the performance of the F.4 was found wanting, particularly so in its rate of climb. Consequently, the unit had F.6s delivered from December 1961. Skirmishes with Indonesian forces over sovereignty issues occurred in 1962, but a United Nations resolution prevented this situation from developing into full-scale hostilities.

Dutch Hunters found it difficult to handle the Indonesian operations because of the enormous flight distances involved. To mitigate this, some examples had additional pylons fitted under their outer wings to enable two more drop tanks to be carried…doubling the F.6's range at altitude from 210 miles to 410 miles (338km to 660km), while still leaving five minutes available for possible combat. In addition, from May 1962 the Hunters began to operate from other bases outside Biak as and when required. The last flights by 322 Squadron on Biak took place on September 15, 1962.

India/Pakistan

Disputes between these neighbouring countries during the 1960s meant the Hawker Hunter was heavily involved in frontline action, taking some losses. This fighting also brought the first occasions when the Hunter participated in what it was originally designed for, air-to-air combat (and in doing so it became the first British swept-wing jet fighter to be engaged in aerial fighting). However, the Indian Hunters' first action came during Operation Vijay, the Indian annexation of Goa in December 1961. Here, 27 Squadron's aircraft were used for strafing runs against airfields and other ground targets.

The Hunter made a substantial contribution to the Indo-Pakistan War of 1965. From August that year, Pakistan became increasingly aggressive in the region of the disputed border with Kashmir. This culminated in a full attack that started on September 1, using heavy armour and with the support of Pakistan Air Force aircraft, specifically the F-86F Sabre. The two closest Indian Air Force Hunter units were 7 and 27 Squadrons based at Halwara, and the first of these flew its initial offensive sorties in this campaign on September 6, losing three Hunters to Sabres

This FGA.9, XF511/F of 208 Squadron, was photographed at Muharraq, Bahrain, in 1967 with the later style of unit decor. (K Prentice via Terry Panopalis)

An Indian Air Force twin-seat Hunter, coded BA360, keeps company with its single-seat equivalent. (Key)

but shooting down three of the latter. Two more Hunters were lost the next day, but they were were also supporting the Indian Army offensive with repeated attacks against ground targets. For example, on September 8, four Hunters employed cannon and rockets to destroy an ammunition train at Raiwind, although another Hunter was brought down by anti-aircraft guns during this operation. Two more Hunters were destroyed on the ground at Halwara on September 14, when Pakistani B-57 bombers attacked at night; on September 16 one Hunter and one Sabre were shot down during an air-to-air battle over Tarn Tarn, and September 20 brought the destruction of two more Hunters.

This conflict, which in the end lasted for 23 days, revealed Pakistan's Sabres were, in some respects, superior to India's Hunters in air combat with the latter apparently losing at least ten against the British design's six Sabre victims. The F-86F Sabre benefited from having Sidewinder air-to-air missiles on board when the Hunter had to rely on just guns. The Sabre could also out-turn the Hunter and the latter did not have self-sealing fuel tanks, which made it an easier target to destroy because of the increased risk of fire. However, India's Hunters performed splendidly as ground attackers, at times carrying substantial war loads deep into enemy territory (an example here was an attack on the Pakistani air base at Sargodha). As the RAF's Hunter pilots had found, the type's 30mm cannon proved highly effective against soft targets and the rockets dealt easily with railway and road vehicles, but they were not quite so successful against enemy armour. A very high proportion of the Indian Hunter sorties were made against ground targets, with most of the remainder being combat air patrol sorties. In the end, however, there were just two occasions in which Hunters and Sabres fought air battles at high altitude.

Hostilities between India and Pakistan broke out again in December 1971, although this time the situation was different for India because it had to deal with an enemy on two flanks. On December 4, Indian Hunters from 7 Squadron again flew raids against targets in East Pakistan (Bangladesh) in response to preemptive strikes made earlier by Pakistan aircraft. Three Hunters were lost but these raids against airfields near Dacca were quite extensive; they included the destruction of a bridge that crossed the River Teesta and the shooting down of three Sabres. However, the situation in the west resulted in 7 Squadron moving to Hinton airbase on December 6, and eight Indian

A Jordanian Hunter gets ready to make its delivery flight from the Hawker factory. (Hawker Aircraft)

The serial of this Indian Hunter F.56 is not sufficiently clear to read, but it's a fine example of this air arm's camouflage and markings on the type.

Hunters were also sent to Nal airbase (that same day a Sabre was destroyed by an Indian Hunter). A Hunter fell to ground fire near Dacca on December 11, and, Indian Hunters from 14 Squadron hit army positions in the district of Dinajpur on the 12th.

To help its forces in the east as Bangladesh was striving for independence, and in an attempt to split India's forces, the Pakistan Army opened another campaign against Kashmir and the Punjab in the west. The Pakistan Air Force's principal interceptors were now the supersonic Soviet Mikoyan MiG-19 (or rather the Chinese-built F-6 version) and the French Dassault Mirage III, but again India's Hunters proved vital in providing ground-attack support. Six Hunters were lost on December 4-5 in raids against various targets in West Pakistan, with just one falling to ground fire. The next day, raids against Pakistan air bases ensured the destruction of more Sabres, along with B-57 bombers, and then from December 7 the Hunters attacked transport, armour and troops but a Sabre brought down one Hunter. Two more Hunters succumbed to ground fire on December 9. The next day brought very heavy fighting on the Munawar Tawi river, and a Hunter was destroyed on the ground at its Pathankot base by a Mirage strafing run. A Sabre and an F-6 were shot down on December 15 by Hunters over the Sind Desert.

On December 17 this bitter war was brought to a halt by a general ceasefire, India apparently having lost 22 Hunters during the conflict, including at least 11 shot down by enemy aircraft. It was evident that in air combat, Pakistan's supersonic fighters held a considerable edge over the by then elderly Hunter.

Arab-Israeli conflict

Two of the main protagonists in the wars between Israel and its Arab neighbours, Israel itself and Egypt, never acquired the Hunter, but examples flown by other nations were dragged into the fighting.

The first major face off was the Six-Day War of June 1967. Here, the Hunters that equipped the Iraqi Air Force played just a small part, but ten were destroyed on the ground, and another five in the air when Israeli aircraft made a surprise attack on Habbaniya airfield. Following this setback, Iraq's Hunters focused on patrolling their country's border, but during the conflict they destroyed a pair of Israeli Sud-Ouest Vautours and one Mirage III fighter.

The Royal Jordanian Air Force had lost a Hunter to a Mirage on November 13, 1966, when four examples tried to counter an Israeli assault on a Jordanian village. With the opening of the Six-Day War

A splendid study of Hunter FGA.9 XT695/K, of 20 Squadron in 1967.

An Iraqi FGA.59. Note the long-range drop tank and retracted airbrake.

the air force was active for just a very short time period. On the first day, June 5, four 1 Squadron Hunters hit an Israeli airstrip at Kefar Sirkin where they destroyed military vehicles and light aircraft. However, all four were then downed by Israeli Mirages on their return to Mafraq, and indeed most of Jordan's Hunter force was subsequently destroyed on the ground at both Amman and Mafraq. On June 6 another Israeli Mirage IIICJ shot down a Lebanese Air Force F.6 belonging to that air arm's 1 Squadron, with the result that Lebanon's aircraft were never again involved in the Six-Day War.

The second major conflict was the Yom Kippur War fought in October 1973. This time Iraq's Hunters were more active and flown to airbases in other Arab countries to provide support. Twelve aircraft from 1(FR) Squadron were deployed to Egypt, but the unit lost three examples on October 8 and another three on the 10th, all shot down by Mirage IIICJs. Another ten went to al-Mazzah in Syria to fly escort for Sukhoi Su-7s on ground-attack duties. In the air, they met Israeli Super Mystères and A-4 Skyhawks but just one Hunter survived, the remainder becoming casualties during intense air-to-air combat or to ground-based anti-aircraft fire/missiles.

Following the 1982 Lebanon War, when Israel invaded the Lebanon in response to constant aggression and counter-attacks between Israel and the Palestine Liberation Organisation, Lebanon's Hunters went into action against Druze militia. However, a number were lost to ground fire or through accidents.

Other air arms

Oman: During the Dhofar War in 1975, Oman experienced increasing incursions into its territory by the People's Front for the Liberation of Oman, a body backed by Yemen. In response, on October 17 the Omani Air Force began to attack guerrilla positions along the South Yemen border and within South Yemen itself, here using bombs and rockets to support ground forces. Prior to November 21, the air strike targets had included rebel hideouts in Hauf. The operations with Oman's Hunters lasted right through to December 2, when the Dhofari insurgency finally came to an end after 13 years with the capture of the last guerrilla-held village at Dhalqut.

Rhodesia: After this country had stated its Unilateral Declaration of Independence from Britain in 1965, its Hunters began flying patrols early in 1966 along the border with Zambia. As a counter, RAF Gloster Javelins of 29 Squadron, based in Zambia, flew patrols on the other side of the border, but ironically both forces had to come under the authority of Rhodesian Air Traffic Control, since this body covered much of Zambian air space.

Later that year, Rhodesia's Hunters performed low-level attacks against Frelimo guerrillas in Mozambique, in support of the Portuguese Government. From 1972, 1 Squadron's Hunters were once again employed against guerrillas, this time attacking camps in Zambia. These latest operations continued until a ceasefire came into effect in December 1979.

Somalia: In the 1980s, Hunters belonging to the Somali Air Force were used against rebel groups opposed to the regime of Siad Barre. However, the air force ceased to operate with the fall of Barre's realm in 1991, and the onset of civil war.

An undated view of a Rhodesian Air Force Hunter, R-1284, at Durban. However, the photo was taken after airframe re-numbering had started. (Key)

▼ Hunter F.58, J-4032, Swiss Air Force aerobatic team Patrouille Suisse, 1991. Dark Green, Dark Sea Grey and aluminium lacquer.

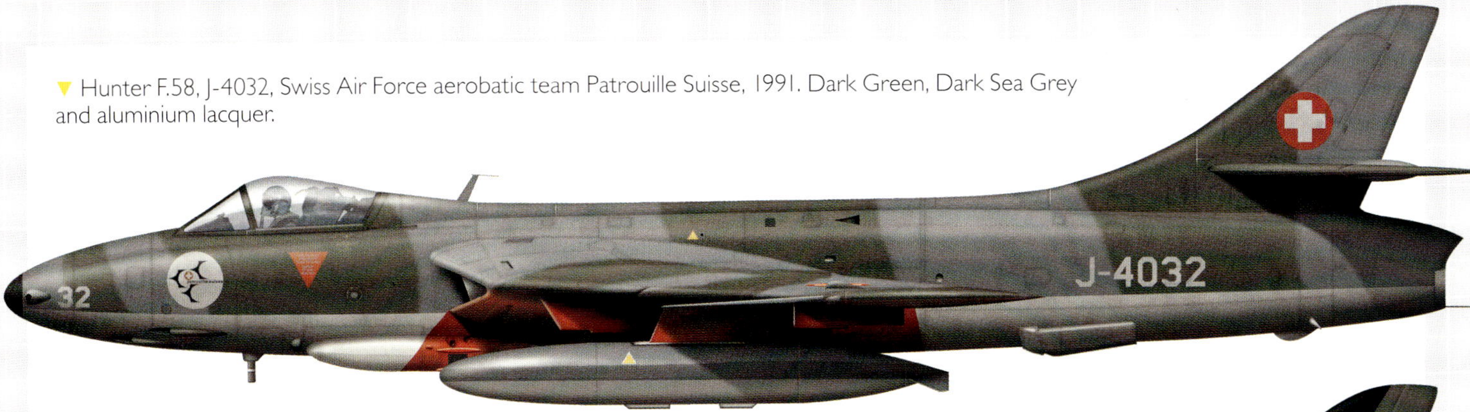

▼ Hunter FR.74B, 545, Royal Singapore Air Force, 1970s. Dark Green and Dark Earth over pale grey.

▼ Hunter F.60, 60-602, Royal Saudi Air Force, 1966. Dark Earth and Middle Stone over medium blue.

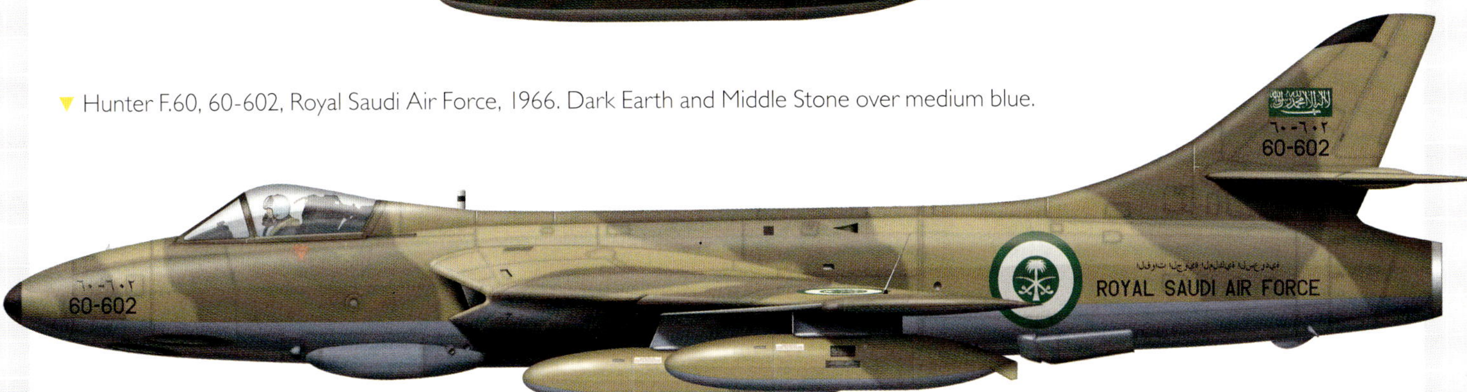

▼ Hunter F.51, E-420, 724 Squadron Royal Danish Air Force, 1970. Dark Green, Dark Sea Grey over High Speed Silver.

▼ Hunter T.66D, S573, 2 Target Tug Flight 'Banners', Indian Air Force, 2001. Dark green and medium grey over pale grey.

(Andy Hay/www.flyingart.co.uk)

North Weald was home to these 111 Squadron Hunter F.4s at the time this photo was taken in 1956. (Key)

SMOKE ON!

The Hawker Hunter was such a superb aircraft to fly that pilots quickly championed it as a stable aerobatic platform.

Indeed, at 1950s Farnborough shows there appeared to be swarms of Hunters, with individual examples demonstrating various weapons options. Unsurprisingly, the type proved to be an excellent mount for formation flying and those events also brought the first appearances of RAF aerobatic display teams. With substantial foreign orders for the aircraft, some overseas air arms also formed their own teams.

United Kingdom

Hunter formation aerobatics began in the UK. The first RAF display team, formed in 1955, came from 54 Squadron, which sent four Hunters (F.1s and 4s) to that year's Farnborough show in September. Subsequently this team was named the Black Knights, not from the colour of their aircraft but due to the pilot's black flying suits. The 1956 Farnborough ushered in a team of four F.4s from 43 Squadron, but in fact for that year (and in 1955) the RAF had two official Fighter Command formation aerobatic teams, with the second on both occasions being the Hunter F.4s of 111 Squadron. As an illustration of their burgeoning skills, in May 1956 'Treble-One' gave a performance at Bordeaux, France, where its complement of four aircraft at one stage made nine simultaneous sonic booms!

For 1957, 111 Squadron, then equipped with Hunter F.6s, took over as the RAF's premier display team, though at that stage they were still to be called the Black Arrows and flew just five aircraft. The CO was Sqn Ldr Roger Topp and in due course their mounts were painted in a splendid black livery. However, it is understood that several black/yellow schemes were trialled before

The 92 Squadron RAF Blue Diamonds perform a 16-aircraft loop. (Crown Copyright)

this final form was selected. One of those rejected was named 'Golden Arrow' by those aircraft spotters who saw and photographed what was an overall black scheme, with a large yellow arrow-headed stripe along the aircraft's fuselage.

The Black Arrows truly made their mark at the September 1958 Farnborough, when they executed a loop of 22 Hunters in formation, a world record which still stands today. Flight reported that to enable 'Treble-One' to get so many aeroplanes together for this history-making achievement, the number was made up with Hunters and pilots supplied by 1, 2, 19, 56 and 92 Squadrons, CFE and 229 OCU. Having completed their famous loop, the Black Arrows then performed (during the same display) the world's first barrel roll made by 16 aircraft in formation. Sqn Ldr Peter Latham replaced Topp in late 1958, and for his two-year tenure in charge he expanded the Black Arrows to a nine-aircraft outfit. Having developed and perfected the art of aerobatic flying by big formations of jet fighters, 111's final Farnborough came in 1960 where it presented an 18-strong 'Pterodactyl Loop' and then manoeuvres with two teams of nine aircraft.

The Black Knights of 54 Squadron at Farnborough in 1955. The Hunters are WW641, WT659 and two F.4s. These aircraft had red and blue wingtips, but later the leader's aircraft (then WW636/Q) acquired a yellow lightning flash on a blue tail and another Hunter (WT692/S) had a blue flash on a yellow tail. (Adrian Balch)

From black to blue

In 1961, Treble-One was replaced by Sqn Ldr Brian Mercer's 92 Squadron as Fighter Command's formation aerobatic squadron. Initially the team was to be called The Falcons, but *Flight* reported this title did: "not appear to have met with general favour". Later the same magazine noted that the team, with its aircraft painted in a splendid royal blue scheme with white wingtips, had been nicknamed The Blue Diamonds by a German newspaper and this stuck (the Black Arrows title was apparently coined by a French newspaper).

The first displays were made on Whit Monday, 1961, during shows held at Wattisham, Hucknall and Yeadon and the performance involved groups of nine, seven and five aircraft. The Blue Diamonds developed new manoeuvres and formations of

The display Hunters of 43 Squadron in 1956: WT641/T, WT613/R and WT587/N. (Key)

The famous 22-aircraft loop is practised by 'Treble-One's', Black Arrows, after they had borrowed Hunters and pilots from several other units. (BAE Systems)

The five-ship Black Arrows team in 1957 or 1958. (Crown Copyright)

their own with plenty of smoke and much use of aircraft breaking away at unexpected moments. By that year's Farnborough in September there was a new formation called the 'Diamond T', in which seven aircraft flying in line abreast (very difficult to do) and another nine in a diamond behind, would perform a complete loop. The routine also involved a 16-ship roll in one large diamond and other manoeuvres with four split sections of four aircraft. T.7s eventually formed part of the team along with the F.6s and the unit also flew displays in Europe. No 92 Squadron continued its formation flying during the 1963 season, but with new mounts… supersonic English Electric Lightnings.

During the 1960s the Royal Navy's Fleet Air Arm expressed a liking for 'humorous' names for its display teams as a counter to the RAF's preference for more 'gung-ho' monikers. De Havilland Sea Vixen teams were formed, called Fred's Five and Simon's Circus, and in the summer of 1965 the Rough Diamonds were formed by 738 NAS. This had four Hunter GA.11s (with a spare aircraft attached) and retained the standard FAA Hunter colour scheme of Extra Dark Sea Grey over white, although the aeroplane flown by team boss Lt Cdr Christopher Comins had Day-Glo red painted on its nose, wingtips and spine.

The Rough Diamonds were disbanded in 1969, but in 1975 a second naval Hunter formation aerobatic team was formed, called the Blue Herons, and again with four GA.11s and with Herons a reference to HMS Heron, in other words Royal Naval Air Station Yeovilton. The team was unique in that all four of its pilots were civilians (working for Airwork Services), though each had military backgrounds (the blue part of the name reflected their previous RAF or Fleet Air Arm experience, with their uniforms traditionally light or dark blue). The Heron's debut display was made at the Yeovilton Air Day on September 6, 1975, and they stayed together performing at major UK shows right through until the end of the 1980 season (one-off performances were subsequently staged at the Yeovilton Air Days of 1984 and 1986).

RAF Germany

Initially, most Hunter squadrons within 2nd Tactical Air Force (2 TAF) in Germany had display teams of their own. These included 20, 26, 93, 112 and 118 Squadrons, and in 1956-57 these units took part in competitions held at the start of these seasons to establish an official aerobatics display team, and a solo display pilot. In 1956, 93 Squadron commanded by Sqn Ldr Desmond Browne, won the team competition while 118 Squadron supplied the solo, and this combination represented the Command at air shows across six European countries. The same combination won again in 1957, 93 then under the command of Sqn Ldr H 'Taddy' Minnis, but this time with Hunter F.6s rather than the Mk.4s

No 92 Squadron's the Blue Diamonds were famous for performing a loop in this formation, 'Diamond T', with seven Hunters line abreast and another nine forming a diamond. (Key Collection)

Four Hunters from 93 Squadron and the solo aircraft from 118 Squadron (centre rear), who in 1956-57 represented 2nd Tactical Air Force at airshows across Europe. (Tony Buttler)

used during the previous year.

There was never an official name for 93's team, which preferred instead to use its squadron identity, but it did introduce new elements in its aerobatic performances. For example, just seconds after retracting the wheels after taking off, one notch of flap would be selected by all pilots and then held throughout the performance until the approach for landing. This gave them a quicker engine reaction and operation with higher revs, which provided the capability to perform a display within a smaller air space. In addition, the acquisition of higher-thrust F.6s in 1957 enabled 93 to take off together in a box formation and then, after clearing the runway, to pull up into a loop and roll off the top to make a low-level return pass over the runway.

The solo Hunter's aerobatics would include climbs, rolls and loops, horizontal and vertical figure-8s using Derry turns, a spectacular inverted break for landing, and at one point a sonic boom from 40,000ft (12,192m). The latter would involve the Hunter diving supersonically to stay ahead of the boom, after which the pilot could enter the display area at subsonic speed and 'beat the boom'; this was intended to make some spectators think that a Hunter could in fact go supersonic in level flight.

The 1957 Defence White Paper brought an end to 2 TAF display teams after the 1957 season. Afterwards, the Black Arrows and Blue Diamonds would visit RAF air days in Germany, and14 Squadron fielded a four-ship F.6 team in 1960.

Overseas air arms

Belgium: The F.6 was the mount used by the Red Devils (or Rode Duivels/ Diables Rouges) aerobatic team first commanded by Maj Robert Bladt. The initially unnamed squad, part of 7 Fighter Wing, gave its first public performance at Valenciennes, France on June 12, 1957. To begin with it flew in standard camouflage before, at Chievres in October 1959, it appeared in a nine-aircraft formation with the lower wings of each aircraft painted in Belgium's national colours (in this display they were accompanied by 16 F.6s in standard colours). Cost-cutting then reduced the team to just four bright-red Hunters in 1960 (with two additional spare aircraft) and this was when the name Red Devils was coined. They performed their last show on June 23, 1963.

Holland: Two Netherlands Air

XE532/L (nose only), XG232/G and then a line of Hunter F.6s, of the Blue Diamonds, pictured at Leconfield in June 1961. (Adrian Balch)

The Swiss Air Force Patrouille de Suisse aerobatic display team. (Key)

A dazzling Hunter F.56 from the Indian Air Force's Thunderbolts team. (Key)

A spectacular photo of Blue Diamonds Hunters in line abreast and climbing to perform a loop. (Adrian Balch)

Force units created Hunter aerobatic teams. The first was 325 Squadron, which ran the 'Darling' display group in 1956-57. The second was 322 Squadron with a team formed in early 1958 on its new Hunter F.4s; it later went on to perform with the F.6.

India: The Thunderbolts aerobatic display group was formed in 1982, specifically for the Indian Air Force's Golden Jubilee. It used nine 20 Squadron F.56As painted spectacularly in dark blue and white. The Thunderbolts continued to display until they were disbanded in 1990.

Jordan: In 1964 the Royal Jordanian Air Force formed a nine-aircraft Hunter team called the Hashemite Diamonds and, as the largest and only nine-ship team ever formed in the Middle East, it performed its first show on November 4. The Hashemite Diamonds continued their displays in 1965 under the command of Flt Lt Hameed Anwar, who was seconded from the Pakistan Air Force.

Peru: For Peru's Aviation Day on September 23, 1956, the air force produced a four-aircraft team called Los Cuatro Ases (The Four Aces), and one speciality that lasted right through until 1961 and its disbandment was to fly routines and to land in rhomboid (diamond) formation. The team was often accompanied by a separate solo display Hunter called El Pájaro Loco (The Crazy Bird).

Sweden: In 1956 a Swedish Air Force aerobatic display team was formed by F 18 Wing with four and later five Mk.50 (J 34) fighters. This was called the Acro Hunters (derived from the English word 'acrobatic') and specialised in 'British-style' displays, with smooth transitions from one formation to another and manoeuvres at low speeds (rather than following the 'American school' with lots of high-speed passes, full power and plenty of noise). The Acro Hunters were led by Sven Lampell and were intially called the Lampell Team. After increasing to five aircraft, they too introduced an indivdual or solo machine to fill in around the main section's formation passes. The team's last public display was on September 1, 1962, then it disbanded and was replaced by the Acro Deltas, equipped with the double-delta-winged SAAB Draken.

A separate Hunter display group was formed by F 8 Wing in 1958, called the Dyrssen Team after its commander Maj Gerhard Dyrssen. In 1959 he was succeeded by Robert Gustavsson who, in 1962, became the last CO for the Acro Hunters. Then for the 1964 season just F 9 Wing established a third and final Swedish Hunter display squad called the Göta Blue Hunters. Another five-aircraft unit, its mounts carried no specific markings and were led by Karl-Henrik Lindespang.

Switzerland: Perhaps the most famous Hunter display team formed outside the UK was the Patrouille de Suisse, founded by the Swiss Air Force in August 1964, with four Hunters. It used the type continuously in its Alpine environment and abroad until 1994, when it transitioned to the Northrop F-5E (though two displays in 1968 had the team flying the Dassault Mirage). In 1970 it was expanded to a five-aircraft unit and then soon afterwards to six. The Patrouille de Suisse proved very popular on its regular visits to the Hunter's home country, particularly to the Royal International Air Tattoos held at Fairford, Gloucestershire.

▼ Hunter GA.11, XF291/789/BY, Rough Diamonds, Fleet Air Arm, 1969. Extra Dark Sea Grey over white, with Day-Glo panels.

▼ Hunter F.6, 111 Squadron RAF trial scheme for Black Arrows, circa 1957. The livery was known among enthusiasts as 'Golden Arrow', but it was rejected for the version finally adopted. Gloss Black, with yellow arrow running from tail to nose, and yellow on the upper wings. It's not known which shade covered the wing undersides.

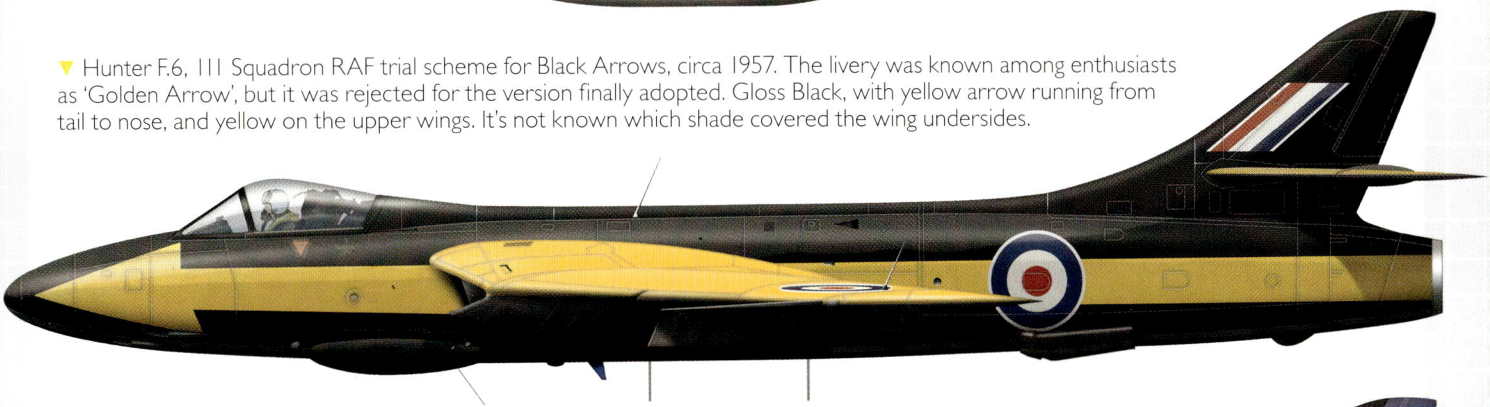

▼ Hunter F.6, XG225/M, Sqn Ldr Brian Mercer, 92 Sqn RAF Blue Diamonds, Middleton St George, 1961.

▼ Hunter F.4, IF70, Diables Rouge, Belgian Air Force, 1977.

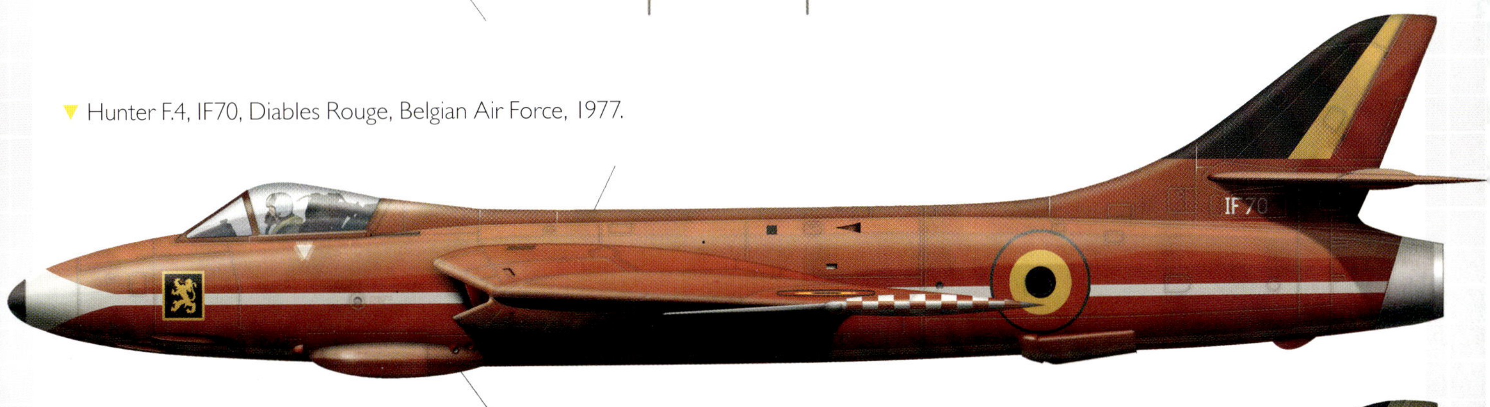

▼ Hunter F.50, 'D', Acro Hunters, F 18 Wing, Swedish Air Force, 1960-61.

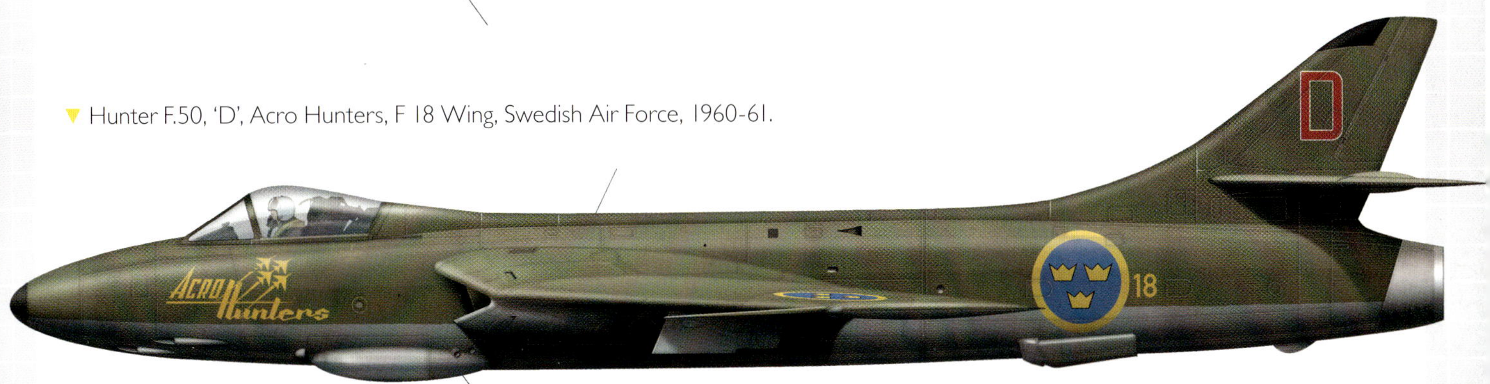

(Andy Hay/www.flyingart.co.uk)

◀ Forward fuselage. Note the small air louvres immediately behind the rear of the canopy.

▼ Bare-metal skinning surrounds the jet pipe. Note the para-brake housing on top.

WALK AROUND

The RAF Museum Hendon has a beautifully maintained Hunter FGA.9, XG154… the subject of this useful detail study

▲ Pylon ejector unit fairing and whip aerial on top of the wing.

▶ This exhibit's cockpit instruments are intact. Note how the paint has worn. (RAF Museum)

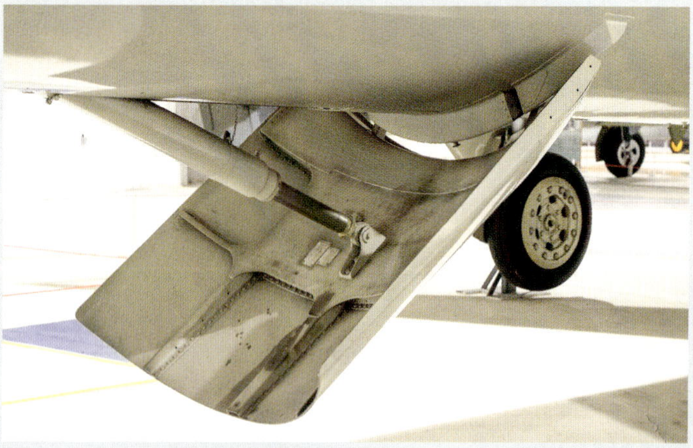

▲ The under-fuselage airbrake in lowered position.

▲ The starboard flap in its lowered position.

◀ Main undercarriage bay. (All Matthew Roberts unless stated)

▲ Port 'Sabrina' link collector and cartridge case ejection ports.

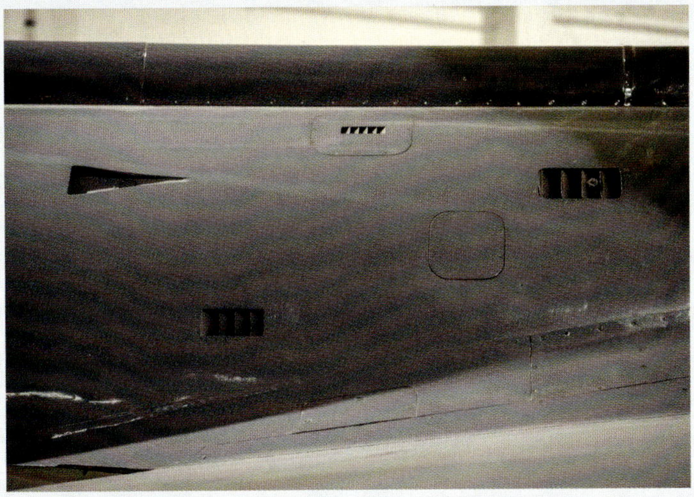

▲ Fuselage features here include the NACA-style engine bay cooling intake (far left) and cooling air outlet (far right).

▲ Starboard main undercarriage.

▲ Nose undercarriage.

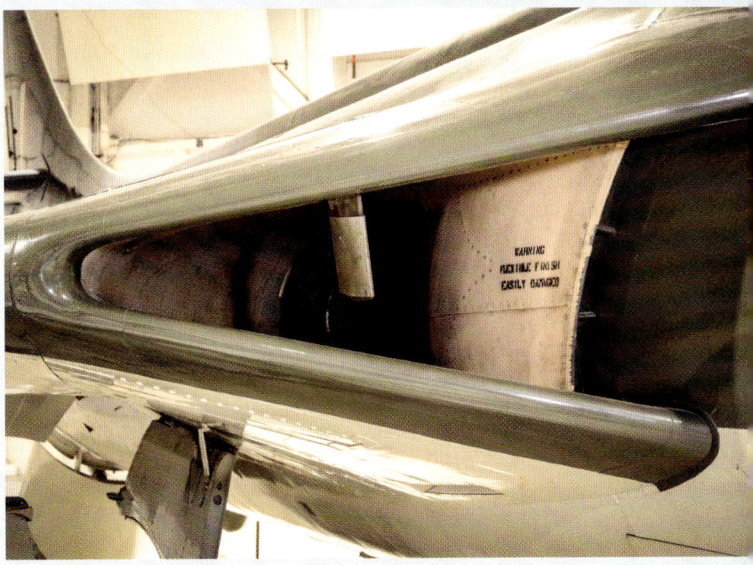

▲ Starboard air intake, with engine facing just visible.

Thanks to the RAF Museum Hendon www.rafmuseum.org.uk/london and Matthew Roberts www.matthewrobertsphotographer.co.uk

OVER THE JUNGLE

Roy Gamblin describes his experience as an RAF 20 Squadron Hunter pilot during the Indonesian Confrontation

The Malaysian Federation was formed on September 16, 1963. It comprised the various states of Malaya, plus Sabah (formerly North Borneo), Sarawak and Singapore. Neighbouring Indonesia had raised violent objections to the plans for the new state. Its chief complaint was the incorporation into Malaysia of Sabah and Sarawak on the island of Borneo, where Malaysia and Indonesia shared a 980 mile-long (1,580km) jungle border. On the day of Malaysia's formation, mobs ransacked the British Embassy in Jakarta; the period known as 'Confrontation' (towards Malaysia) had begun for real. Actions by Indonesia soon escalated and included seaborne guerrilla landings in Johore, and attacks in Sarawak, Sabah and Singapore. Over the following years, Indonesian Air Force bombers made threatening flights over the town of Kuching in Sarawak and carried out air attacks on Malaysian villages in Borneo. Indonesian paratroopers were dropped in the jungles of Johore. Confrontation finally came to an end with the ratification of the Bangkok Accord between Indonesia and Malaysia in August 1966. Singapore had left the Federation on August 9, 1965 to become an independent Republic under Prime Minister Lee Kuan Yew.

During Confrontation, a very large defensive presence of British, Australian and New Zealand armed forces was based in Malaya, Singapore and Borneo under the obligations of the member nations of the South East Asia Treaty Organisation

A 20 Squadron Hunter FGA.9 patrolling the Malayan jungle in 1965.

Hunter FGA.9 XJ685/R is photographed by the author over the Malay Peninsula. Note the deployed airbrake and empty rocket rails under the wings.

(SEATO). The bulk of the British forces were based on the island of Singapore, where the RAF had three large and busy airfields...Changi, Seletar and Tengah. Changi was the main transport aircraft base, while Seletar hosted helicopters and lighter transport aircraft.

Tengah was home to 20 Day Fighter/ Ground Attack (DFGA) Squadron, equipped with 16 Hunter FGA.9s and two T.7s. Disbanded at the end of 1960 in RAF Germany, the squadron had reformed at Tengah in 1961 in response to a concern that SEATO might have to react to Communist aggression in Laos. 20 Squadron remained at Tengah until the general withdrawal of British forces from the Far East began in 1970. The busy airfield was shared during Confrontation with two resident RAF Canberra units, (45 with B.15 bombers and 81 with recce aircraft) and two resident Javelin all-weather fighter squadrons, 60 and 64. At the height of Confrontation, Tengah temporarily accommodated 14 Squadron of the Royal New Zealand Air Force (more Canberras), a disembarked Fleet Air Arm Sea Vixen squadron (for a short period while its carrier was repaired in Singapore), a rotating detachment of Vulcan or Victor bombers from the UK or Cyprus, and occasional detachments of Royal Australian Air Force Sabres from their main base at Butterworth near Penang.

Groundcrew pose for the camera on the flight line at Tengah, in the mid-1960s.

New blood

Into this busy, exciting, vibrant, colourful, noisy, hot and steaming tropical milieu, a young RAF Flying Officer arrived at Changi, sleep-starved, at about 0830hrs one morning in the middle of October 1964, after a 27-hour journey from the UK in an RAF Britannia via Istanbul and Bombay. It was six weeks after my 20th birthday. I was to join 20 Squadron, having graduated as a teenage Hunter pilot following 2 1/2 years' RAF pilot training, culminating in three wonderful months at the Hunter Operational Conversion Unit at RAF Chivenor, Devon.

Just before I left the UK, there had been front-page stories in the newspapers reporting the actions of 20 Squadron's Hunters against Indonesian guerrillas, who had landed in Johore and who were being fought on the ground by British troops. I was ready (or so I thought), and certainly eager, to join in the action and adventure with little thought for the dangers. After all, as a young fighter/ground-attack pilot, I had been imbued with a sense of invincibility (perhaps better described as over-confidence in view of my inexperience as an aviator, not to say life in general). However, I was very soon to hear that any more action, when and if it came, was only for the experienced operational pilots on the squadron. Meanwhile, I would become firmly absorbed for the time being into the ranks of the 'JPs', the junior pilots yet to complete their in-theatre operational training on the FGA.9 before being allowed out against the foe.

The Hunter was of course an absolute delight to fly, and I had totally revelled in the training at Chivenor. My very limited ambitions at that time simply did not extend beyond that of being a Hunter pilot, ideally for eternity. I was completely absorbed in my exciting role. Flying a fast and agile aircraft, pointing it frequently at the ground at 400kts or more, loosing 3in rockets at targets on the air-to-ground ranges at Asahan, near Malacca, or Song Song Island north of Butterworth, and firing one, two or, very rarely, all four of the 30mm Aden cannon (directly underneath the seat in my high-speed, 6g 'office'), usually at ground targets and sometimes at the hessian 'flag' towed behind a Meteor, was an endlessly thrilling and hugely satisfying encounter.

In fact, we very rarely got to fire the four Adens together because it was both expensive and unnecessary, other than to prove the system occasionally and to provide each pilot with at least one experience of the multiple effects of firing a full pack. Those results included tremendous noise, and such vibration that circuit breakers popped out all over the cockpit, often in the rear area that was hard to reach if you were bulky or tall like me. There was also the rapid, Newtonian deceleration (in reaction to 80 9oz (250g) projectiles being expelled forward every second at a muzzle velocity of 1,807mph (2,900km/h). When firing four Adens, the Hunter lost 50 to 60kts airspeed in seconds. I imagined anything more than a two-second burst would have caused the sturdy aeroplane to pop all its rivets - but it didn't when I tried it one day with the full six seconds.

Mark-one eyeball

The routine of training from Tengah naturally included many low-level navigation and visual reconnaissance exercises, at 250ft over the dense jungles of the southern Malayan mainland. Mock attacks were made on a wide variety of ground targets, often bridges, which were always filmed for later analysis on the ground to assess their likely chance of success. The attacks were conducted normally in pairs or fours of aircraft and, to provide extended range, often included a high-level outbound and return cruise at around 35,000ft, skirting the cumulonimbus clouds that normally rose to much higher altitudes by mid-afternoon. Very occasionally, we had the opportunity to make simulated attacks against Royal Navy warships. Those allowed us the opportunity to make

The personnel and aircraft of 20 Squadron pose for the unit's 50th anniversary in 1965, at Tengah, Singapore.

exciting low-level passes across the ships, not always using the most tactical of parameters. The navy often encouraged a 'beat-up'.

The day-fighter role provided further scope for exciting and interesting training. That began with basic fighter-to-fighter combat techniques involving just two aircraft, matched one against the other, then progressed to 2 v 2 or 2 v 4 exercises. In air combat training, we practised offensive and defensive techniques to improve our abilities to build the essential 3D mental picture, which enabled us to spot the opportunities early enough to get into a position to 'kill' the other aircraft. Air combat training was usually flown high above the jungle or the sea and involved much rapid rolling and pitching at high G, in very tight vertical and horizontal manoeuvres with many rapid reversals; heads swivelled constantly to maintain visual contact with, or search for, the prey. Our G-suits were almost permanently inflated, squeezing the trunk and legs to prevent blood pooling in the lower limbs and body, while we enhanced our G threshold by tensing our stomach and neck muscles as hard as we could, grunting and sweating like mad and frequently wiping rivers of sweat out of our eyes. We had always started off very hot and sweaty anyway on the ground before take-off in the tropical heat and high humidity, and the Hunter's cooling system was often not adequate enough to cool us down from the metal cockpit's oven-like ground temperature before the gymnastics began. We returned to earth frequently dehydrated, yet soaking wet in our thin, lightweight Australian flying suits, which rotted quickly as a result and had to be changed regularly for new.

When in air combat as a pair against another pair or four, it was the main role as a JP to fly as a 'wingman', in loose, swept formation at about 250–300 yards (230-270m) from the pair's leader and act as the rearward eyes of the section. One had to pay prime attention to sticking in the correct position on the leader as he manoeuvred hard, while constantly twisting and turning one's neck to the rear to confirm our tails were clear of any threat. It was of course equally important to keep tabs on all the other, 'friendly' aircraft involved. Mid-air collisions could easily occur in air combat training; they did happen and were usually fatal. Over the following years I lost numerous friends in such accidents, though not during my 20 Squadron tour.

Badger threat

Fighter v fighter air combat training was one thing, but we also had to train for the possibility of interception and attacks against the Indonesian *Badger* jet bomber aircraft that were a threat to Malaysian territory. Practice interceptions were made with help from the Ground Controlled Interception (GCI) and air defence radar at Bukit Gombak, on a hilltop on Singapore. The GCI controller was responsible for vectoring us into a position behind the 'enemy' aircraft, usually another Hunter, from which a 'guns kill' could be made. Unlike our Javelin colleagues, with their air-to-air

In this light-hearted view, aircrew relax on a Hunter and the pilot astride the canopy wields a sword, echoing the weapon carried by the eagle on the official 20 Squadron badge.

Wg Cdr Roy W Gamblin AFC (1944 -)

1960-62: Scientific Assistant, Naval Air Dept, RAE Bedford; sea trials on Royal Navy and Indian Navy aircraft carriers, observer flights in Gannet, Sea Vixen and Meteor

1962-64: RAF pilot training, Jet Provost, Gnat and Hunter

1964-67: 20 Squadron at Tengah, flying DFGA Hunters over Borneo and the Malay Peninsula, during the Indonesian Confrontation

1968-70: Loan service with the Sultanate of Oman's Air Force during the Dhofar War; 2 1/2 years in transport and ground-attack roles, flying Beavers, armed Piston Provosts, Dakotas and Strikemasters. Sultan's Commendation Medal

1970-74: Central Flying School course then Gnat Qualified Flying Instructor and Flight Commander at RAF Valley for a three-year period

1974-76: On exchange duty for two years with a Royal Norwegian Air Force F-5A 'Freedom Fighter' squadron

1976-79: OC Standards Squadron, Valley, during the introduction to the RAF of the (then) Hawker Siddeley Hawk (plus a notable Gnat forced landing at Llanbedr in Sept 1977). Awarded Air Force Cross

1979-81: RAF Advanced Staff Course, Bracknell then Plans Branch at Headquarters Strike Command

1982-84: Last RAF post as OC Operations Wing (Harrier) at Wittering

1984-2000: Various commercial roles, plus a year at Llanbedr on the Hawk, Canberra and Devon. More than 11 years with the Civil Aircraft Division of British Aerospace (BAe), Jetstream/ATP/146/Avro RJ, airline training captain, examiner, demonstration pilot, test pilot and project manager. Much time with customer airlines worldwide including the USA, Caribbean, Europe, Turkey, China, Bangladesh, Indonesia and New Zealand. Presented with BAe Chairman's Award for Innovation

missiles, we just had our Aden cannons and so we had to get within roughly 600 yards (550m) to ensure success. It was a process of skilled teamwork for pilot and controller, especially as the initial approach was normally from an offset, head-on position. The timing and execution of the 150- to 180-degree turn into the target aircraft's rear sector required great precision by both parties.

However, the *Badger* had a radar-controlled tail-gun so it was not a good idea just to arrive leisurely behind it at the same height and just 600 yards. Therefore, a special technique known as a 'snap-up' attack was developed and practised by Hunter pilots, to enable us to spend the very minimum amount of time behind the target, having achieved a shooting position rapidly and unexpectedly. The method called for us to be vectored just into the target's line astern, 2,000-3,000ft below it, with an overtake speed of about Mach 0.05. We would wait until we were almost directly below the target, head craned back to see him almost vertically above, and then ease our aircraft into a climb, changing to a bunt at a suitable point, from which we would be able to rake the target aircraft with cannon shells as it passed through the gunsight, with the expectation of making the kill before the tail-gun could be operated.

Guerrillas were again landed in November and December 1964 in Johore, near Kota Tinggi and south of Pontian. My operational colleagues were in action against the forces near Pontian on December 23 and again on Boxing Day. In February, March and April 1965 the squadron flew armed escorts for Belvedere helicopters carrying troops into the Kota Tinggi area, to hunt the guerrillas. A further landing of 24 Indonesian soldiers occurred at the end of May, this time on the east coast of Johore, just seven miles from Changi. Once again, four 20 Squadron Hunters were in action on May 31 when, with rockets and cannon and under the aegis of a forward air controller, they dislodged the enemy troops and allowed ground forces to complete the defeat of the intruders over the following days. The JPs, of course, did not get a look-in. However, I was eventually declared fully fit for the fray and dispatched to Kuching in Sarawak to join the regular border patrols flown by detachments of Hunters from 20 Squadron and Javelins from 60 and 64 Squadrons.

I flew for my first time to Borneo as a passenger in a Bristol Freighter (or Bristol 'Frightener' as it was jocularly known) of 41 Squadron, RNZAF. I was a little puzzled before engine start when the Kiwi loadmaster distributed wads of cotton wool to the passengers, who promptly began stuffing it firmly into their ears. I thought this might be some corny joke or even a wry Antipodean custom. However, the reason soon became clear as the twin engines burst into life with an almighty, clattering noise. It took approximately 2 1/2 hours to fly the 408nm (755km) from Changi to Kuching. The sensation was rather like sitting in a giant metal dustbin, while a dozen amateur steel band players

Armed to the teeth: A 20 Squadron Hunter carrying 3in rocket projectiles and 230 gal wing tanks. In front is the Aden gun pack with its ammunition.

This Hunter T.7, XF310, was one of two kept on strength for refresher training and as 'hack' aircraft.

beat the hell out of it from the outside with metal clubs. The noise for that length of time was totally shattering, even with the cotton wool!

Cargo protection

In early 1965, several 20 Squadron Hunters were detached to Kuching in Sarawak to take over fighter escort duties (for supply dropping transport aircraft) from the Javelin squadrons, which were often short of serviceable aircraft. The Javelins suffered from structural airframe cracking and problems with their twin Armstrong Siddeley Sapphire engines - or 'time-bombs' as we cocky young wags on 20 Squadron referred to their troublesome powerplants.

We flew our low-level patrols as two or three aircraft together and participated in exercises with the Army from their border encampments. At the time of my early detachments to Kuching and later Labuan, the available aerial maps for Borneo were very poor indeed. Huge areas consisted of little more than a white sheet on which rivers alone were marked. There were no terrain contours, nor even spot heights shown, although the terrain was often up to 5,000ft above sea level in Sarawak and much higher further north in Sabah. In 1966 better maps became available but, until then, we virtually made our own as we went along. Pilots would come back from low-level flights into the hinterland or along the border, having spotted some previously un-noted significant terrain feature, and plot it on the master map on the crew-room wall. We others would then transfer the data to our own personal maps. I still have these nostalgic mementos.

Although the border areas were generally better marked on the maps, the boundary itself often did not conveniently follow the terrain. Accurate visual navigation along the border was very difficult at times, yet it was essential, particularly in western Sarawak, as it seemed the Indonesians had sited their air-defence guns just on their side of the border opposite where the terrain was most indistinct. We lost no fighters to ground fire, but an RAF Whirlwind helicopter did get shot down in October 1965 on the border south of Kuching, after getting

Personnel of 20 Squadron scramble to their aircraft at Tengah. Note the Roman 'XX' on the nosewheel door of the nearest Hunter. (Key)

too close to one of the Indonesian anti-aircraft guns.

We flew low-level navigation exercises eastwards along the great muddy brown Rajang and Bateh rivers, the latter with huge jungle-clad mountains soaring to several thousand feet barely a mile to either side of us and ending where the Indonesian border turned from parallel to our track, then to cut directly across it in a spectacular, green, mountain-fringed dead-end. Clear weather at the mountain ridges was rare, so we usually needed a steep, full-power climb out at the end of the cul-de-sac, into cloud, to clear the ridge-tops. Wingmen like me had to tuck quickly into close formation before the leader entered the cloud and then be ready to fly through heavy rain, and often hail, bucking about like a wild horse in the turbulence as we fought to stay in close formation in marginal visibility, and U-turned to fly back to Kuching, 250nm (400km) to the west.

My first session in Borneo lasted two weeks before I returned to Tengah to re-join the ongoing routine training over Malaya. The squadron celebrated its 50th anniversary in August 1965 and, apart from the social celebrations on the ground, the occasion was marked by a 16 aircraft flypast at RAF Tengah, in which I flew as number six.

On September 1, 1965, two Indonesian Air Force B-25 Mitchells strafed a small Malaysian village close to the border in Sabah and about 100 miles (160km) south of the RAF airfield on Labuan island. As luck would have it, four 20 Squadron Hunters had been sent to Labuan two days earlier to take part in an exercise, and so these aircraft were immediately tasked to patrol the border area to deter or shoot down any further airborne intruders.

Then, on September 17, a further three FGA.9s, with the second aircraft flown by me, were sent to Labuan to enable the Air Commander to increase the patrol rate. A further six Hunters flew out to Labuan from Tengah the following day. At the height of the three-week attempt to deter or shoot down intruding Indonesian aircraft, we flew a continuous daylight patrol along a very large stretch of the jungle border in the north. To allow us the maximum time on patrol, each of our aircraft was fitted with two outboard 100 gal (450 lit) drop tanks, and two standard inboard 230 gal (1,050 lit) tanks. Flying at best range speed to and from the patrol areas, and then at endurance speed while patrolling the border, we were able to stay airborne for just over two hours at low level.

Early flight

My first patrol, the day after arriving at Labuan, involved a take-off soon after dawn. It was typical of the many flights that followed on these 'special patrols'. We headed south-southeast from Labuan, on much the same heading as the runway, to coast in at low level within four minutes after take-off over the mangrove swamps of mainland

A fully armed 20 Squadron Hunter during the Indonesian Confrontation.

Hunter FGA.9, XJ683/F, 20 Squadron, Tengah, Singapore, 1965 (Andy Hay/ www.flyingart.co.uk)

Borneo, and then to our patrol area a further six minutes and 35 miles (56km) away. As we flew south over the jungle in the early light of the day and in the gathering heat, steaming mists rose all around us out of the jungle canopy like huge columns of smoke from a volcano…a stunning sight. As we flew on, we climbed steadily with the rising, densely tree-covered terrain to nearly 6,000ft. We kept a listening watch on the Army radio frequency from which we heard occasional, and usually outdated, calls relating to further suspected Indonesian incursions.

In fact, despite these intensive and continuous low-level daylight patrols, often shared with our Javelin colleagues, we never did catch an enemy aircraft. Had we done so, we would have been greatly disadvantaged by the fact that, for political reasons, we were supposed to ensure any enemy aircraft we might shoot down had to fall on our side of the border, to avoid being accused of incursions into Indonesian airspace. Occasionally, we thought we were onto something and the leader would call 'Buster!', whereupon both pilots would select full thrust, accelerating the aircraft rapidly from the patrol speed of around 240kts to whatever we could get, usually around 500-550kts, as we raced to the reported area invariably to find it empty of any threat. The period of special patrols continued for about three weeks and, in that period alone, I logged 43 hours' flying, all at low level above the wide green jungles of Borneo, apart from one 3 1/2-hour round trip over the South China Sea to Tengah and back, to change an aircraft. We normally flew 20-25 hours a month, so I'd rather hogged it.

The routine continued well into 1966; squadron training from Tengah interspersed with operational detachments to Kuching for patrols over Borneo. I had not fired a single shot in anger throughout Confrontation by the time it ended in August the same year, but neither had most of my colleagues, since there were very few instances of our Hunters being in action against ground targets and none against air assets.

In May 1967, shortly after a most enjoyable five-day air exercise when I was detached with the squadron to a tented camp at Gong Kedah airfield, northeast Malaya, by the beautiful tropical beaches up there, I returned to the UK to take up my next job as an instructor at the Hunter OCU at Chivenor. So ended my first operational tour, flying Hunters over the jungles of the Far East at a time when Britain's armed forces were much larger, and flying was much less regulated, simpler and terrific fun. The experience of that first tour in Hunters over the jungle was a fantastic beginning. It became the launch pad from which I then sought the more unusual and more interesting jobs, though not always getting those I'd planned. I moved on in due course to further operational tours in desert and arctic theatres, and was lucky enough to become an airliner captain, trainer, examiner and test pilot operating globally.

Canberra B.15s of 45 Squadron also shared the ramp with 20's Hunters at Tengah.

▼ Hunter F.6A, XE601, Aeroplane & Armament Experimental Establishment, Boscombe Down, Wiltshire, 1990. Light Aircraft Grey and Signal Red.

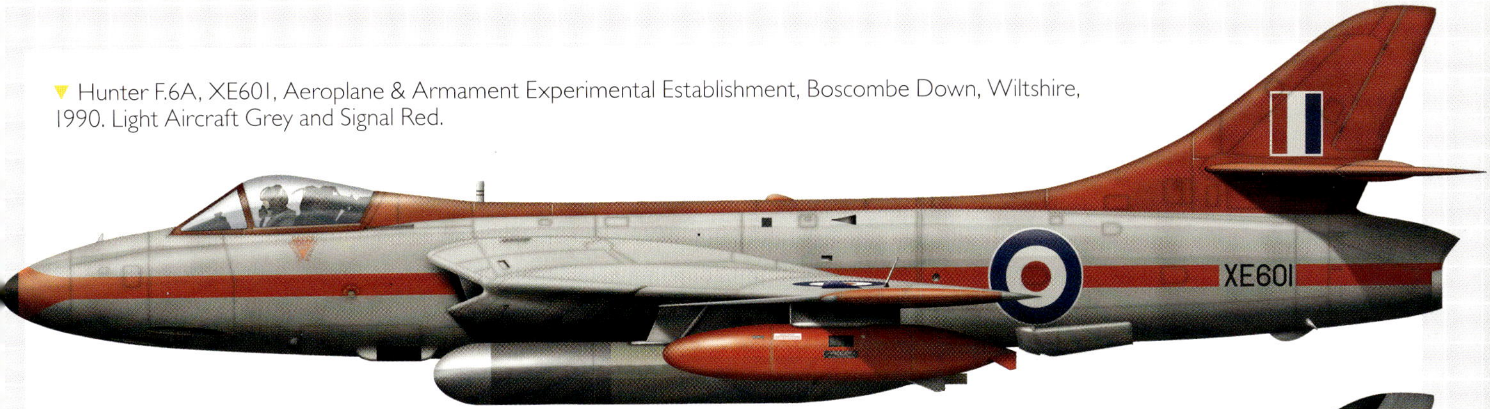

▼Hunter F.6, XF383, 12 Squadron RAF, Lossiemouth, Scotland, July 1984. Dark Sea Grey and Dark Green wrap-around camouflage.

▼ Hunter F.6 XG239/MH, Sqn Ldr Mike Hobson, 92 Squadron RAF, as seen at Armament Practice Camp, Hal Far, Malta, January 1958. Dark Green, Dark Sea Grey and Light Aircraft Grey, with white wingtips.

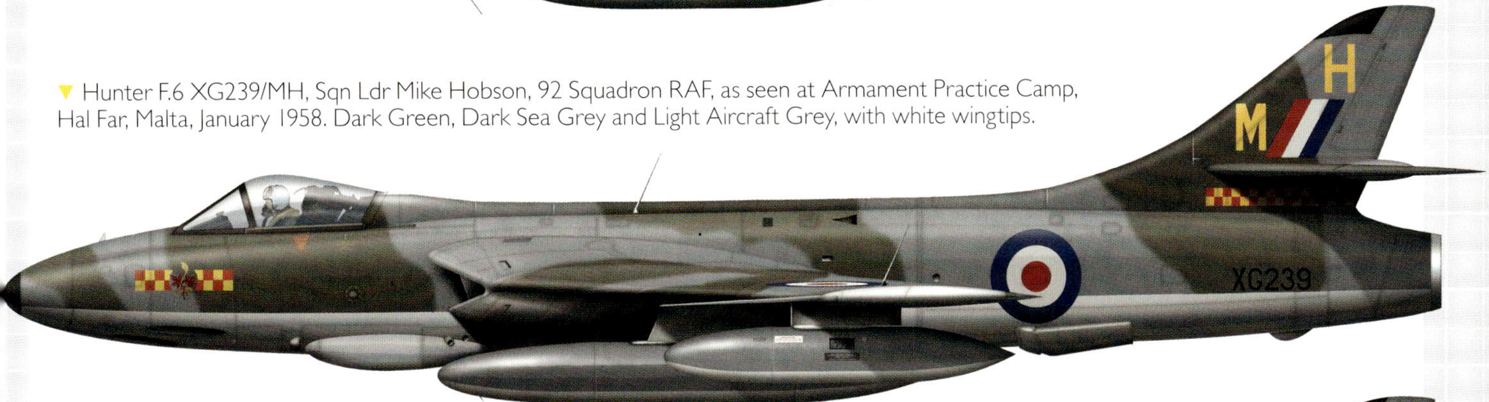

▼ Hunter F.6 XK142/H, 74 Squadron RAF, Coltishall, Norfolk, 1959. Dark Green, Dark Sea Grey and High Speed Silver.

▼ Hunter F.6, XF383/R, RAF Day Fighter Combat School (formerly Day Fighter Leaders' School), Stradishall, Suffolk, 1961

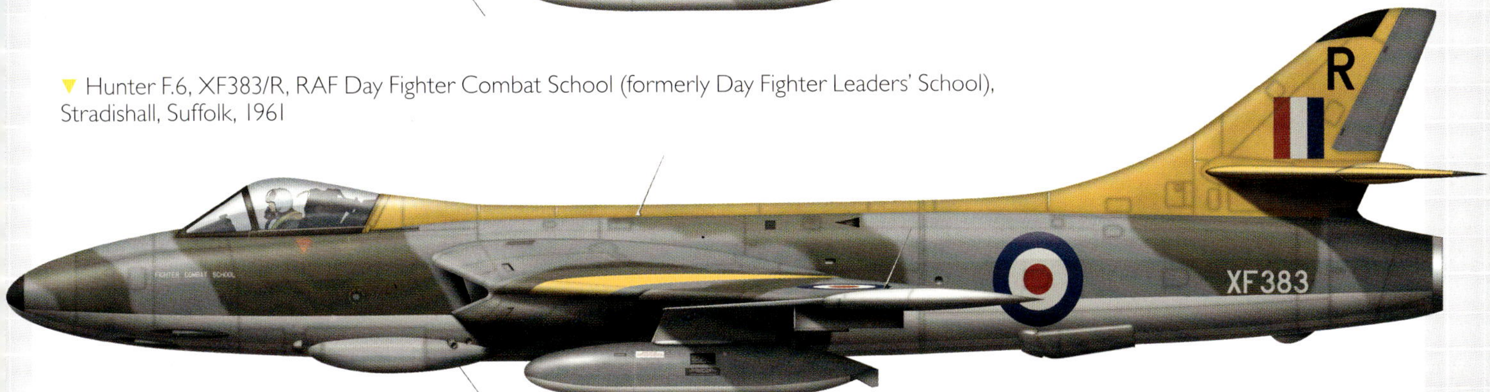

(Andy Hay/www.flyingart.co.uk)

This handy guide to Hawker Hunter kits, decals and accessories concentrates mainly on items currently available. Older products, such as the original Airfix 1/72 Hunters, can still be found via auction sites and at model shows, but we have chosen not to list them here. The list is not definitive.

Airfix's 1/48 Hawker Hunter F.6 built by Andy Davies (*Airfix Model World* - December 2018 issue)

KITOGRAPHY

KITS

1/144

Mark I Models

14480 Hunter FR.10/F.71A/FGA.73A

14481 Hunter T.7

14482 Hunter T.8B/T.8C

Revell

04039 Hawker Hunter FGA.9

Whirlybird Models

WPX44001 Hunter T.7 RAF 4 FTS/234 Sqn, RDanAF

WPX44002 Hunter T.8/T.8C Royal Navy

1/72

Eastern Express

72272 Hunter Mk.1 (ex-FROG)

Extrakit

72013 Hunter T.7

Mister Craft

040116 Hunter 'Maverick Hunter' F.Mk.58

Olimp Models

7250 Hunter T.8M

Revell

04186 Hawker Hunter FGA.9/Mk.58

04350 Hawker Hunter F.6

03908 Hunter FGA.9 100 Years RAF

1/48

Academy

12312 RAF & Export Hawker Hunter F.6/ FGA.9

Airfix

A09185 Hawker Hunter F.6 (new tool)

Italeri

2772 Hunter F.6/FGA.9 Aerobatic Teams (ex-Acad)

1/32

Revell

04703 Hawker Hunter FGA.9/Mk.58

04727 Hawker Hunter F.6

ACCESSORIES

1/144

Master

144019 FGA.9 pitot tube (Mark I/Rev)

Peewit

14015 Hunter T.8B/T.8C masks (Mark I)

1/72

Airwaves

72082 FGA.9 details

Armory

72408 Hunter weighted wheels (various)

Barracuda

72213 Martin-Baker Mk.4 ejection seat

Blackbird Models

BMA72020 F.1/2/4/5 conversion

Brengun

72017 Step ladders for Hunter/Harrier

Eduard

SS230 Hunter F.6 Zoom detail set

CMK

7123 F.6/FGA.9/Mk.58 interior (Rev)

7124 F.6/FGA.9/Mk.58 exterior (Rev)

7125 F.6/FGA.9/Mk.58 undercarriage (Rev)

72099 Hunter mainwheels (Rev)

Eduard

CX105 Hunter F.6 masks (Rev)

Freightdog

72042 Hunter F.4 conversion (Rev)

72080 Hawker P.1130 conversion (Xtrakit)

72100 Hunter T.12 conversion (Xtrakit)

Flightpath

72067 Hunter detail set (Rev)

72204 Hunter access ladder and FOD guard set

LF Models

72093 Hunter T.7 conversion (Rev)

72094 Hunter T.8M conversion (Rev)

Master

72021 Hunter pitot tube

Montex

Hunter F.6 masks (Rev)

Odds & Ordnance (Alley Cat Models)

72014 Hunter two-seat trainer conversion (Rev)

72020 Hunter airbrake detail/correction (Rev)

72023 Hunter T.66/G-APUX conversion (Rev)

72031 Hunter engine intake large detail set (Rev)

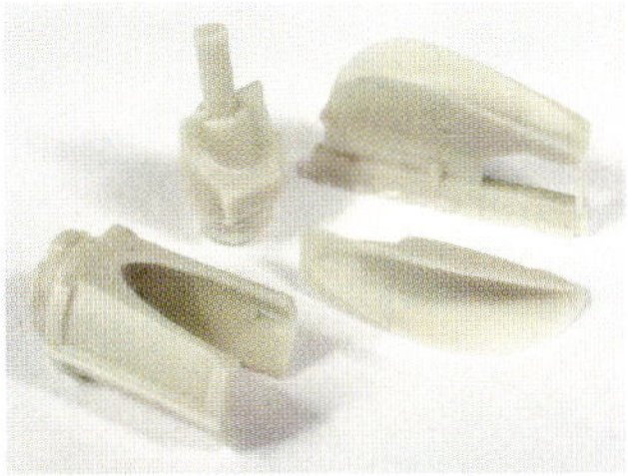

72035 Hunter PR.10 conversion (Rev)

72030 Hunter T.8M conversion (Rev)

Pavla

72049 Hunter F.6 cockpit/vacform canopy

72039 Martin-Baker Mk.3H seat for Hunter F.6/FGA.9

72068 Hunter prototype conversion (Rev)

72089 Hunter Mk.3 conversion (Rev)

PJ Production

721207 Hunter T.7/T.8/T.68 conversion

721208 Martin-Baker Mk.4 seat

Quickboost

72115 Hunter FGA.9 airbrake (Rev)

72129 Hunter clear recce nose (Rev)

72435 Hunter ejection seat

Rob Taurus

72027 Hunter F.6 vacform canopy

Scale Aircraft Conversions

72049 Hunter FGA.9/Mk.58/F.6 landing gear (Rev)

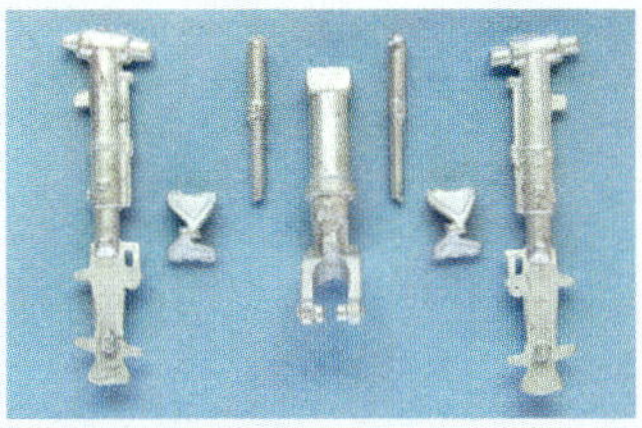

Whirlybird Models

WBA44001 Hunter F.4 wings

WBA44002 Hunter small fuel tank set

1/48

Aires

4805 Hunter F.6/FGA.9 cockpit (Acad)

4087 Hunter F.6/FGA.9 wheel bay (Acad/Ital)

4310 Hunter F.6/FGA.9 details (Acad/Ital)

Armory

48406 F.6/FGA.9 wheels (Acad)

Brengun

72017 Step ladders for Hunter FGA.9/Harrier

Eduard

EX045 Hunter F.6/FGA.9 masks (Acad/Ital)

48233 F.6/FGA.9 details (Acad/Ital)

Falcon

4084 RAF Pt.2 vacform canopies, inc Hunter (Acad/Ital)

Flightpath

48056 RAF Hunter F.6/FGA.9 detail/weapon set (Acad/Ital)

Maestro Models

4818 Hunter F.6/FGA.9 vacform canopy (Acad/Ital)

Master

32035 Hunter FGA.9/F.58 pitot tube

PJ Production

481211 Martin-Baker Mk.4 seat

Quickboost

48550 Hunter F.6/FGA.9 seat (Acad/Ital)

Scale Aircraft Conversions

Hunter F.6/FGA.9 landing gear (Acad/Ital)

SBS Model

48018 Hunter F.6/FGA.9 detail set (Acad/Ital)

Squadron

9596, vacform canopies, inc Hunter (Acad/Ital)

True Details

48423 Martin-Baker Mk.2H seat

49007 Hunter F.6 cockpit

1/32

Blackbird Models

BMA32001 Hunter F.1/2/4/5 conversion (Rev)

Eduard

JX025 Hunter FGA.9/Mk.58 masks (Rev)

Fisher Model and Pattern

Hunter T.7 nose conversion

Hunter T.8M nose conversion

Hunter T.8C nose conversion

Flightpath

32003 Hunter FGA.9/F.58 detail set (Rev)

32004 Hunter FGA.9/F.58 diorama set (Rev)

32005 Hunter F.4/F.5/GA.11 conversion (Rev)

HAD Models

232006 Hunter FGA.9/F.58 wheel set (Rev)

Montex

48206 Hunter F.6/FGA.9 masks (Acad/Ital)

Scale Aircraft Conversions

32014 Hunter FGA.9/F.58/F.6 landing gear (Rev)

True Details

32453 Hunter FGA.9/F.58/F.6 cockpit (Rev)

DECALS

1/72

Airdecal

7211 Raspberry Ripple Fixed Wing Pt.1 (inc Hunter T.7)

Blackbird Models

BMD72038 RAF Hawker Hunters Pt.1

Italeri's 1/48 Hawker Hunter FGA.9 built by Chris Jones (*Airfix Model World* - November 2016 issue)

Airfix's 1/48 Hawker Hunter F.6 built by Andy Davies (*Airfix Model World* - December 2018 issue)

BMD72039 RAF Hawker Hunters Pt.2

Fantasy Printshop

72-001 Hunter Single Seater

72-002 Hunter Twin Seater

72-003 Hunter FAA Single and Twin Seater

Flevo Decals

72005 RNethAF Jet Trainers, inc Hunter T.7

Modeldecal

026, inc Hunter FGA.9

028, inc Hunter T.8

086, inc Hunter F.4/F.6/FR.10

Model Alliance

72136 Senior Service Hunters

72188 RAF Germany, 1970-75 Pt.3, inc Hunter T.7A

72196 RN Aerobatic Teams, inc Hunter GA.11

Print Scale

72336 Hunter FGA.9 RAF

Xtradecal

X72047 Hunter FGA.9/FR.10

X72058 Hunter F.6

X72106 RAF 74 (Tiger) Squadron, inc Hunter F.4

X72123 Hunter T.7

X72124 History of RAF 19 Squadron, inc Hunter F.6

X72148 Hitsory of 4 Squadron, inc Hunter F.6

X72149 RAF 1 Squadron 100 Years, inc Hunter FGA.9

X72150 RAF 2 Squadron history, inc Hunter FR.10

X72214 International Hunters

X72278 Suez Campaign 1956, inc Hunter F.5

1/48

Blackbird Models

BMD48011 RAF Hawker Hunters Pt.1

Colorado 48099 Gulf Air Power 1991/2, inc Oman Hunter

Dutch Decal

48071 Hunter F Mk.4/Mk.6/T.7 KLu/RNethAF

DP Casper

48012 Arabian Hawker Hunter F.6/FGA.9 Six Day War 1967/Yom Kippur War 1973

Fantasy Printshop

48-001 Hunter Single Seater

48-002 Hunter Twin Seater

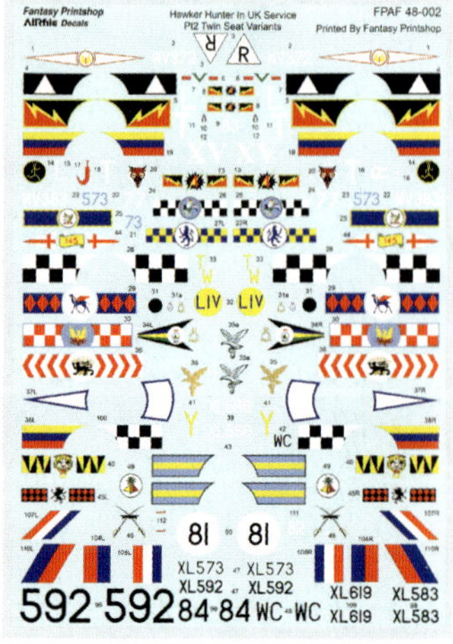

Freightdog

48010 Hunter F.4 RAF Germany

Model Alliance

48136 Senior Service Hunters

48188 RAF Germany, 1970-75 Pt.3, inc Hunter T.7A

48196 RN Aerobatic Teams, inc Hunter GA.11

Xtradecal

X48033 Hunter F.6

X48034 Hunter FGA.9/FR.10

X48105 Hunter F.6/FGA.9

X48107 100 Years of 4 Squadron, inc Hunter F.6

X48108 100 Years of 1 Squadron, inc Hunter FGA.9

X48189 Hunter F.6

X48191 Hunter Mk.6 Pt.2

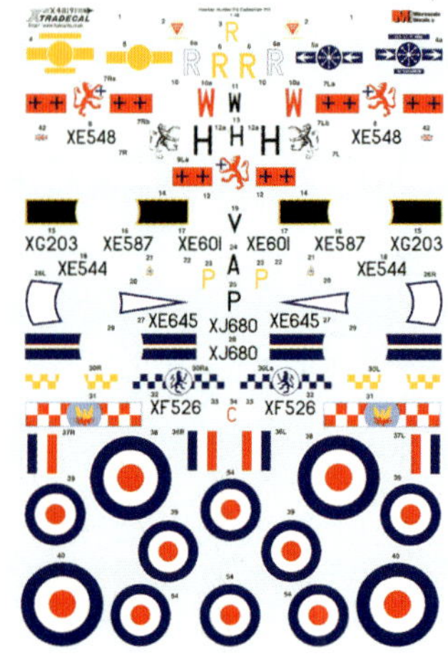

X48192 Hunter F.6 Pt.3

1/32

Blackbird Models

BMD32001 RAF Hawker Hunters Pt.1

Dutch Decal

32029 RNLAF Sabre and Hunter

Fantasy Printshop

32001+ Hunter roundels

32001++ Hunter serials

32002 Hunter serials

32001 Hunter Single Seater

32002+ Airfile Hunter roundels

32-002 Hunter Twin Seater

Flevo Decals

32004 RNethAF Jet Trainers, inc Hunter T.7

Linden Hill

32005 Iraqi Fighters, inc Hunter F.6/F.59A